MW01195904

Ships of the Great Lakes
An Inside Look at the World's Largest Inland Fleet

Patrick D. Lapinski

Enthusiast Books

Enthusiast Books
1830A Hanley Road
Hudson, Wisconsin 54016 USA

www.enthusiastbooks.com

Library of Congress Control Number: 2011923766

ISBN-13: 978-1-58388-280-1
ISBN-10: 1-58388-280-4

Reprinted February 2014

Printed in China

IN MEMORIAM
*
Richard M. Seymour
1947-2010
*
We dedicate this book to our friend, leader and partner. He will be deeply missed.

Table of Contents

Dedication

To my travel companion and son Sam for his wit, wisdom and energy; to Pete, that he always knows the value of perseverance, and to Deb for encouragement, support and countless prayers that we always return home safely.

Acknowledgements

This book would not have been possible without the support and contributions of a number of friends, maritime historians and individuals. Their contributions of information, images, proofreading, and support throughout the project have been invaluable.

Bill Peterson, Keylakes Shipping; Tom Wiater, Central Marine Logistics; Christine Rohn-Tielke, Interlake Steamship Company; Kathy Elinski, American Steamship Company; Lucio Odorico, Compass Minerals; Jeff Himes, Ray LeClair, Carmeuse; Fred and Laurie Heaunalt, Voyageur Marine Transport; Ed Wiltse, Marc Rohn, Grand River Navigation; Seaway Marine Transport; Canada Steamship Lines; Lower Lakes Towing Ltd.; Vanguard Shipping; Capt. William Yowell; Capt. Raymond Sheldon; Capt. Vaughan Kendall; Capt. Joe Ruch; Capt. Jeremey Wonk; Capt. Pat Nelson; William Burnett.

About The Author

Patrick Lapinski, a native of Superior, is a researcher, writer and photographer concentrating on the Great Lakes maritime industry. The author's photography and writing has been featured for many years in Great Lakes publications such as the Duluth Seaway Port Authority's *North Star Port*, *Great Lakes Seaway Review*, the Lake Superior Marine Museum Association's *Nor'Easter*, the Great Lakes Historical Society's *Inland Seas*, *Lake Superior Magazine*. To see more imagery and writing, look to the website: www.inlandmariners.com

INTRODUCTION:
Great Lakes Ships at Work

It is important to understand the history of these lakes, if only to fully appreciate the tradition to which we belong. The Great Lakes are deeply steeped in the history of the North American continent. Their waters circumvented a thickly wooded interior to become the only viable trade route. Over their clear, cold surfaces traveled the tireless voyageurs—the energetic missionaries followed by the cautious settlers. It is a region that has grown from hardship, sacrifice and courage to become uniquely adapted to its fresh water environment.

The arrival of European's to the Great Lakes region came with the stroke of a canoe paddle; a fine blade of wood serving as sleight of hand for the beginning of a new era of life along the lakes and rivers set deep within a nearly impenetrable continent. Maritime commerce officially began on Lake Ontario in 1679 with the 45-ton barque of *Le Griffon* and the 10-ton *Frontenac*. *Le Griffon* became a legend; not for what it was, the first ship, but for what it didn't do, return. *Le Griffon* is the most sought after shipwreck on the inland waters, a ship destined perhaps to never be found. Since then, many have followed, some sharing a similar fate while others forged the links to the past we look upon today with admiration and wonder.

The Great Lakes maritime industry has moved far beyond anything comparable to those early years of exploration and commerce. Changes even in the recent half-century have obliterated much of what was considered advanced technology two generations ago. But, technology alone is not the only benchmark we can use to examine today's Great Lakes mariner.

Sailing wasn't thought of as an educated man's job, as a career that one aspired to. It was a step between what could be done with a strong back, without a modicum of education. Sailing was a job where young men tested their entitlement to adventure, of going to sea, even though on the Great Lakes it meant rarely being outside the sight of land. In many aspects of our society the sailor is still looked upon as some sort of cultural miscreant, a person void of the skills needed to succeed in modern society.

Education and knowledge are highly prized attributes of today's mariners. The majority of sailors today are graduates of maritime academies. They are highly educated in the hard skills of sailing; navigation, electronics and engineering. Additionally, they are trained in areas of people skills; performance management, team work, and customer service. In an era of reduced manning on vessels every member of the crew is expected to contribute, many performing cross-functional duties (Assistant Cook combining 2nd Cook and Porter duties; General Purpose Maintenance Rated, combining deckhand and wiper) combining the functions of jobs that were separate positions less than a generation ago.

Over the past two hundred years the industry has matured. Long-standing trade routes have been established but within those routes the customer face has changed. Traditional, long-term contracts to haul iron ore now extend no more than a decade, if that. Steel companies that once operated their own ships hauling exclusively for their mills have divested themselves of this practice. Those same ships are now competing for cargoes on the open market. Increased rail competition has made major inroads in the Canadian grain trade, taking advantage of year-round movement. On the positive side, an upswing in the movement of stone and aggregates for the construction industry, and the development of the low-sulfur, western coal market has created new opportunities for the Great Lakes maritime industry.

The images and text that follows examines the activity that occurs throughout the Great Lakes every shipping season. It is an epic story defined by action, formed by movement, and carried out by the interaction of machinery and human labor; of Great Lakes Ships at Work.

CHAPTER 1:
Ships of the Great Lakes

Merchant ships on the Great Lakes are roughly divided into categories determined primarily by their size and the type of trade they are involved in. For the purposes of this book, the strict use of vessel classification standards followed by insurance underwriters such as Lloyds of London, or the American Bureau of Shipping is not necessary. If you are an ardent student of marine engineering, seaworthiness, and existing admiralty laws this may be an area of interest to pursue.

When it comes to the maritime industry, size grabs our attention; from the *Titanic* and *Lusitania* to the *Queen Mary 2* in passenger liners to merchant vessels like the *Sinclair Petrolore* in the 1950s, *Berge Stahl* in the 1980s to the *Emma Mærsk* launched in 2006. The Great Lakes shipping industry is a perfect example of this "size is better" equation. The breakthrough came in the late 1800s with the development of steel shipbuilding, setting the tape measures in motion. First came the 400-foot ships, then 500, and by 1900 ships of 600 feet in length were showing up on the drawing boards at shipyards around the Great Lakes.

Almost every era in shipbuilding on the Great Lakes in the past 150 years has been devoted to increasing the overall dimensions of the ship. You couldn't call it a conspiracy, for no one owner consciously sat down with his competition in a dusty mold loft room at the shipyard with a fastidious plan to outdo another. Economy of scale is what they sought to attain so that they could remain competitive within their industry. When the new lock at the Soo is completed it could again lead to increases in vessel size.

On the lakes, 730-foot vessels are the norm, and ships exceeding 1,000 feet in length are common. Vessels of 600 feet, once considered giants, are now rather "smallish" in comparison. The larger of these carriers are used to move massive loads of iron ore and coal down from the upper lakes (Lake Superior) to the steel mills and power plants on the lower lakes (Lakes Michigan and Erie). In any given season these giants each haul upwards of 3 million tons of cargo. There are currently 13 thousand-foot vessels on the Great Lakes.

Throughout its career the *Indiana Harbor* has been a record-setter for the American Steamship Company. The vessel has set records for the largest shipments of iron ore, coal and limestone, and is also the only thousand-footer to have carried grain. The *Indiana Harbor* is dedicated to the western, low sulfur coal trade with occasional cargoes of iron ore.

Canadian-owned 730-foot Seaway-sized bulk carriers transport grain harvested on the Canadian prairies for distant ports on the St. Lawrence Seaway. The ratio between distance and cargo capacity make these lakers ideal for this trade. In comparison to truck and rail transportation, moving bulk cargo by ship is still the most economical mode.

Self-sufficiency is possibly the most notable hallmark of today's Great Lakes shipping industry. Nearly every vessel afloat is equipped with self-unloading technology, allowing vessels to discharge their cargoes day or night without the necessity of shore side equipment or manpower. This change in operational process has allowed the industry to service its customers more cost effectively, with higher efficiency.

The *American Spirit*, operated by ASC, was originally built for National Steel and operated for many years as the *George A. Stinson*. From 1992 to 1997 the vessel was operated by Interlake Steamship. The vessel was re-named the *American Spirit* in 2004.

This section will take a look at the types of vessels representative of those working on the Great Lakes. It is not intended as a compendium of every vessel in existence on the lakes. Rather, the intent is to show the functionality and efficiency of the ships at work and the markets in which they trade.

The *Walter J. McCarthy Jr.* was built specifically for the low-sulfur coal trade between Superior, Wisconsin, and St. Clair, Monroe or Essexville, Michigan. The *McCarthy* is seen here departing the harbor at Duluth-Superior with a load of coal destined for one of Detroit Edison's power plants. The *McCarthy* carries an average of 62,000 tons per trip.

The *Stewart J. Cort* was the first thousand-foot vessel built for use on the Great Lakes. The *Cort* is currently operated by the Interlake Steamship Company. The *Cort* rarely deviates from its weekly delivery of iron ore pellets from Superior, Wisconsin, to ArcelorMittal's Burns Harbor steel mill. The downturn in the national economy left the vessel in long-term lay-up for the duration of the 2009 shipping season.

One of the unique features of the *Cort* is its hydraulic hatch covers. The vessel was designed to only haul iron ore and does not have the cubic capacity to economically carry coal or stone. The ballast tanks for the *Cort* are controlled from the deck by the mate on duty, rather than relying on the engine department to pump the ballast water during loading.

Between 1976 and 1977 the American Shipbuilding Company at Lorain, Ohio, built two 1,000-foot vessels for the Cleveland-based Interlake Steamship Company. The *James R. Barker* and the *Mesabi Miner* are each 1,004-feet long by 105-feet wide and service both the coal and iron ore trades, carrying over 3 million tons annually.

The *Paul R. Tregurtha* is the largest vessel on the Great Lakes at 1,013 feet in length. The *Tregurtha*, the reigning Queen of the Lakes, operates primarily in the low-sulfur coal trade from Superior, Wisconsin, to ports on the St. Clair River and the lower lakes. The vessel was built in 1981, its aft end and a portion of the cargo hold constructed at Lorain, while the bow and the remaining cargo hold were built at Toledo.

The *Edgar B. Speer* loads primarily at the ore docks at Duluth and Two Harbors; occasionally loading at Superior, Silver Bay, or Escanaba for U.S. Steel's mills at either Gary, Indiana, or Conneaut, Ohio. The *Speer* is equipped with a side-extending shuttle boom, which limits the docks where the vessel can unload. In some circumstances the *Speer* will moor alongside another vessel and off-load its cargo ship-to-ship with the receiving ship discharging the cargo onto the dock with its longer reaching deck boom.

Entering the Poe Lock is the 1000-foot *Edwin H. Gott*. The *Gott* was the first of two "thousand-footers" built for U.S. Steel's Great Lakes Fleet. In 1995 the *Gott* was refitted with a 280-foot deck boom, the longest on any lake vessel. The *Gott* was built to haul iron ore exclusively and makes runs from Lake Superior to steel mills along the lower lakes at Nanticoke, Detroit, Gary, Conneaut, and Indiana Harbor.

One of the most easily identifiable vessel profiles belongs to the ITB (Integrated Tug-Barge) *Presque Isle*. The *Presque Isle* is the only 1,000-foot tug-barge combination on the Great Lakes. Unlike an ATB (articulated tug-barge), the ITB is designed to operate as one unit, meaning the tug is not able to sail functionally independent of the barge unit. Built as a prototype, the ITB process did not catch on with other lake fleets.

The construction boom of the 1980s brought a new class of vessel to the Great Lakes. The smaller "river class" of ships are designed to be self-maneuverable to carry products into small ports and docks on a seemingly never ending schedule moving coal, stone, sand and iron ore. M/V *Manitowoc*

These river class ships are 630 feet in length and 68 feet wide. They will usually load to the water draft of the dock they are bringing cargo into. Typical loading ports for these ships are Port Dolomite, Port Inland, and South Chicago on Lake Michigan, Port Calcite and Stoneport on Lake Huron, and Silver Bay on Lake Superior. M/V *Calumet*

All three vessels were sold in 2006 to the Wisconsin and Michigan Steamship Company (although none of these are steamships) when the Oglebay Norton Company phased out its Great Lakes marine division. In 2008 the vessels were acquired by Rand Logistics and then re-sold in a baseball-like deal that included ships and cash to the Canadian firm of Lower Lakes Towing, of Port Dover, Ontario. M/V *Robert S. Pierson*

The *American Republic*, built in 1981, is 634 feet, 10 inches in length and has a cargo carrying capacity of 24,000 gross tons. The *Republic* is the ultimate river boat, built with two standard rudders and six additional "flanking" rudders to increase maneuverability. The vessel makes frequent shuttles carrying iron ore between Cleveland's lakefront dock to ArcelorMittal's steel mill up the Cuyahoga River. In 1995 the ASC-GATX billboard was painted on the hull when the vessel participated in the Olympic torch relay.

The *Adam E. Cornelius* is named in honor of one of the founders of the modern day American Steamship Company. This is the fourth vessel to carry the name in the fleet's storied history. The *Cornelius* was the first of the river class vessels built for use on the lakes. At the time it was named the *Roger M. Kyes*. The *Cornelius*, 680 feet long, is seen here departing the Duluth harbor with a load of coal from Superior's Midwest Energy Terminal.

At 636 feet in length, the *American Courage* was built for the river trade; in particular, the Cuyahoga in Cleveland, and the Saginaw. One characteristic of this style of vessel length is their narrow beam, which makes it easier for them to make the turns and twists of the rivers. The *American Courage* was acquired in 2006 by the American Steamship Company.

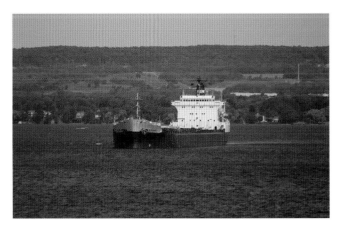

The long, sleek shape of the bulk carrier is synonymous with the Canadian grain trade, traveling the waterborne route from the grain terminals of Lake Superior to ports along the St. Lawrence Seaway. The Seaway class bulker *Canadian Provider*, known in Canadian lakes vernacular as a "flat back," passes down-bound on the St. Clair River. M/V *Canadian Provider*

Just as the American Great Lakes fleets converted their ships to self-unloading capability to service the ore trade, the Canadians continued to embrace the bulk carrier for their Seaway customers. These lakers feature large, deep cargo holds that are ideal for carrying grain, a commodity that requires a large cubic capacity. M/V *Algonorth*

The *Pineglen*, the former flagship of the Paterson lakes fleet, approaches the Tower Avenue slip at Superior's Cenex-Harvest States elevator. The vessel operates exclusively in the grain trade for Canada Steamship Lines. In 1996 the *Pineglen*, then operating as the *Paterson*, set the U.S. record for the largest cargo of soybeans when it loaded 28,941.6 tonnes at the Superior elevator.

The *Algocape*, inbound for Canadian National's Duluth ore dock, is managed by Seaway Marine Transport. While trading primarily in Canadian grain, the *Algocape* occasionally takes cargoes of iron ore to mills along Lake Ontario and up the St. Lawrence Seaway. Without a self-unloading boom it will take longer to unload the vessel, but with its deep cargo hold the vessel can carry a considerable amount of cargo.

In its colorful blue livery the *J. W. Shelley* departs Superior with a cargo of ore pellets. The *Shelley,* owned and operated by Vanguard Shipping of Canada, is the former *Algocen*. The vessel was taken off the lakes for use as a disposal barge along the East Coast but has returned to ply the ore and grain trade.

The *Montrealais* pours it on, heading up the St. Clair River to Thunder Bay, Ontario, for a load of grain. It takes about five to seven days one-way, or about two weeks round-trip for a bulk carrier to load, deliver the cargo, and return. In deference to the time it takes to make a round trip, bulk transportation by ship is still more economical than rail and truck.

Seaway sized self-unloaders now comprise the majority of the Canadian Great Lakes fleet vessels. Many are newer ships, built during a period of upgrade during the 1980s. Vessels, such as the *Canadian Transport*, were constructed to service the Canadian coal-fired power generation industry. The *Transport* is seen here being assisted up the St. Louis River at Duluth to discharge a cargo of road salt.

With its distinguished name and its impressive dimensions of 740 feet in length and a width of 78 feet, the *Rt. Hon. Paul J. Martin* is maximized to fit through the locks on the St. Lawrence Seaway. Operated by Canada Steamship Lines, the *Martin* carries coal to generating stations at Lambton and Nanticoke, and ore to customers at ports along the St. Lawrence River.

The *John D. Leitch* is a rather unique, and at the same time awkward, looking vessel with its tall forward deckhouse and living accommodations. The *Leitch* is one of a large pool of Canadian self-unloading vessels managed by Seaway Marine Transport. The *Leitch* operates in the coal and ore trade and is seen here arriving through the Duluth ship canal for a stop at Superior's Midwest Energy Terminal.

There is not likely a more seafaring sounding name than that of Captain Henry Jackman. While the name embraces the Algoma Central Marine sailing tradition, the vessel is an ultra-modern ship with its raked bow and stair-stepped after cabins. The self-unloader *Capt. Henry Jackman*, built in 1981 as the *Lake Wabush*, glides purposefully down the St. Clair River with a cargo of coal.

It is believed that once a vessel enters the salt trade that it has less than a decade left in its career. Algoma Central Marine's *Algomarine* may be a prime example of this adage. The *Algomarine* frequently loads salt at Goderich, Ontario, for delivery to ports along Lake Michigan, such as Milwaukee and Chicago. The vessel is seen here up-bound in the Detroit River. The *Algomarine* was originally owned and operated by Nipigon Transports Ltd., a joint venture of Hanna Mining and the commodities firm of Cargill.

The *Canadian Ranger* is one of the more unique looking self-unloaders on the lakes because of its fo'csle-mounted unloading boom. The *Ranger* is seen here entering the Duluth harbor on a stormy summer afternoon. There is a wonderful story surrounding a family of raccoons who found a home for the winter on the conveyor belt only to be unceremoniously "put ashore" when the conveyor system was tested before the start of the next shipping season.

The evolution on the Great Lakes of the articulated tug barge (ATB) has extended the life of a growing number of older American steamers. By removing the forward cabins and aft engine spaces and then utilizing the un-manned cargo hold section powered from behind by a tug, shipping companies are able to avert the expense of building a new ship. The *Joseph H. Thompson Jr.* (tug) and its consort *Joseph H. Thompson*, is one of the earliest applications of ATBs on the lakes.

The tug *Jane Ann IV*, paired with its barge *Sarah Spencer*, is a former ocean-going tug purchased for use on the lakes. This ATB combination is unique because the *Spencer's* original pilothouse was left intact when the hull was notched for use as a barge. In this case, the pilothouse on the un-manned barge is equipped to steer the vessel while being powered from the tug, removing the need to create a raised pilothouse for the tug. The *Sarah Spencer* usually operates in the Canadian grain trade.

The *Great Lakes Trader* and its tug *Joyce L. Van Enkevort* were built in 1998 for use on the lakes, rather than adapting a tug to work with an older hull. The *Great Lakes Trader*, at 740 feet, was constructed in Mississippi and the tug was built in Sturgeon Bay, Wisconsin. The ATB is frequently employed hauling stone on the lower lakes, and in the Lake Superior iron ore trade.

The *Pathfinder* and its tug *Dorothy Ann* marked the first entrance in recent years of a major Great Lakes shipping firm into the world of the ATB. The barge *Pathfinder* is the hull of the former Interlake Steamship Company steamer *J. L. Mauthe*, built in 1953. The *Mauthe*, never lengthened or converted to a self-unloader, was an ideal candidate for pairing with a tug once it outlived its efficiency as a bulk carrier.

Looking forward from the starboard side of the *Dorothy Ann* shows where the tug fits into the notch on the barge. The tug has a pair of rams that fit into a series of teeth on the port and starboard sides of the barge unit. The horizontal alignment of the rams allows the tug to move independently of the barge while underway and is also adjustable for the loaded draft of the barge. The ability to move independently from the barge is the primary difference between an ATB and an Integrated Tug Barge, where the tug and barge move as one unit.

Looking down the notch wall on the starboard side of the barge *Pathfinder* gives a good view of the "teeth" that connect with the tug unit. The rams extend out from each side of the tug and lock into the teeth of the barge. The white markings are used to make it easier to be sure the tug and barge are equally aligned on both the port and starboard sides.

The *Roger Blough* and the *John G. Munson* are representative of several generations of the long storied history of U.S. Steel's once powerful Great Lakes Fleet. The *Blough* was supposed to be the first thousand-footer on the Great Lakes but trepidation on the part of fleet engineers resulted in a modified 858-foot vessel when it was launched in 1972. The *Blough*, fitted with a shuttle boom, operates exclusively in the iron ore trade between Duluth or Two Harbors, and Gary, Indiana, or Conneaut, Ohio.

The *John G. Munson* has been openly characterized as a "money maker" on the lakes. Long, swift and versatile, the *Munson* easily fits the description of a tramp steamer, carrying multiple cargoes of iron ore, limestone and coal up and down the Great Lakes, fitting into large and small ports. The *Munson* is seen here up-bound (light) on Lake Huron for Stoneport.

The *Clarke, Anderson*, and *Callaway*, the three "AAA" class ships of the once enormous U.S. Steel fleet, have all followed a similar evolution as lakers. The *Clarke*, the first of the three vessels built in 1952, was lengthened 120 feet at the end of the 1974 season and was converted to a self-unloader at the completion of the 1982 season. The *Clarke*, seen here departing Two Harbors, generally works in the iron ore, stone and salt trade.

The *Arthur M. Anderson*, like its sister ships, still trades heavily in the movement of iron ore, but, after U.S. Steel divested itself of its majority interest in the lake fleet, the *Anderson* and its fleet mates began openly competing for cargoes against other fleets rather than hauling exclusively for U.S. Steel. Since then the *Anderson* has been actively engaged in the shipment of stone and coal as well as iron ore.

The *Cason J. Callaway,* while similar in outward appearance to its fleet mates, underwent an automation of its engine room at the end of the 2001 season, becoming the first steamship on the Great Lakes to be controlled directly from the pilothouse. The ultimate goal of this automation was to reduce operating costs, such as fuel consumption. Additionally, automation brings about a reduction in manning of the engine room. The automation was engineered by the firm of G. R. Bowler while the *Callaway* was at Fraser Shipyard, Inc. in Superior, Wisconsin.

At 806 feet in length the *Charles M. Beeghly* briefly held the distinction as the longest steamship on the Great Lakes. In 2009 the *Beeghly* was converted to a diesel-powered vessel. The conversion is part of an overall plan by Interlake Steamship to upgrade its aging steamers to make them run more efficiently, and to be in compliance with new federal emissions standards. It has been estimated that the conversion cut the ship's daily fuel consumption by over fifty percent.

The *Lee A. Tregurtha*, a former World War II tanker, continues to be a workhorse in the Interlake fleet of ships. The *Tregurtha* regularly loads iron ore from ports along Lake Superior for delivery to steel mills on the Rouge River and at Indiana Harbor, while backhauling coal from Lake Erie and Lake Michigan northward for the power generating industry. The *Lee A. Tregurtha* is 826 feet in length and is seen here gliding gracefully across Lake Superior on a serene summer day.

The elegant steamer *Kaye E. Barker* passes through the Neebish Channel with a load of iron ore destined for Severstal Steel on the Rouge River. The *Barker* regularly loads at Marquette for the Rouge and then loads eastern coal at either Toledo or Sandusky for delivery to power plants along Lake Michigan before returning to Lake Superior. The *Barker* also loads taconite at Escanaba for ArcelorMittall's Indiana Harbor steel mill.

While not the largest cargo carried on the lakes in terms of tonnage, the movement of powdered cement is vital for use in the upper Midwest construction industry. Nearly all of the steamers once actively involved in the cement trade have been replaced by modern tug-barge combinations. The *Alpena* remains as one of the few steamers still making the rounds of the Great Lakes. In fact, the *Alpena* is a survivor—the last "AA" class vessel built in 1942. In 1989 the vessel was shortened 120 feet to its present length of just over 519 feet for use in the cement trade.

Spring navigation begins in mid-March at the head of the lakes. While ice conditions in ports like Duluth-Superior have a reputation for being difficult, spring and winter navigation on the lakes usually faces its biggest challenge in the connecting rivers below the Soo Locks. Here, the *John J. Boland* is making its way out of Fraser Shipyard to begin another season while an already loaded *Cason J. Callaway* trails behind.

CHAPTER 2:
The Fire Down Below: The Engine Department

For those mechanically inclined or just curious, the engine room is like no other place on a ship. The engine room straddles several layers of the ship, starting at the bilge and ending just below deck level. To the uninitiated, an engine room is a complex area. It can be loud, hot, and filled with things in motion. Machines turn on unexpectedly, sirens and alarms are output at high decibel levels, and a wide variety of liquid lubricants can make bumping into something an unpleasant experience.

The engineering department on a Great Lakes ship is charged with keeping all things mechanical on the ship in operating condition. This comprises several main areas, including the propulsion system; electrical generation for ship's house; the ship's HVAC system; plumbing and sanitation, including the kitchen and housekeeping equipment; and all of the machinery on the deck, such as winches, the hatch crane, hoists, windlasses, and the unloading system.

Within the engine room proper, the ship's main propulsion system encompasses the main engines, whether steam turbine, or diesel; the reduction gear(s); and the propeller shaft(s) and propeller(s). The majority of merchant vessels on the Great Lakes are powered by diesel engines. Small to medium sized ships usually have two to four main engines. When underway, they may only operate three of them to save on fuel, while alternatively, they may operate all when maneuvering. The engines vary in power based on the size of the vessel. A thousand-footer powered with four 20-cylinder engines will produce around 16,000 horsepower, while a ship with smaller 8-cylinder engines may only produce half of the output. Diesel-powered engine rooms are highly automated with systems designed to be operated with minimal manpower.

On a steamship, the engineers have to maintain the ship's boilers in addition to the turbine engines. The boilers heat water to produce the high pressure steam that feeds the turbines. When maneuvering in port or in the rivers the boilers may be lit-off multiple times, requiring an engineer manning the throttles and monitoring the boilers. On the Great Lakes today there are less than two dozen steamships still in

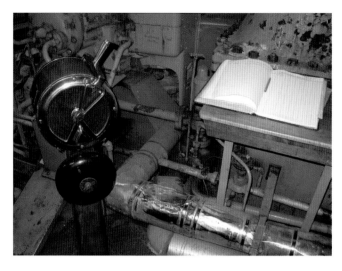

The radio telegraph, also known as the Chadburn, is the main line of communication between a steamship's engine room and the ship's pilothouse. When the ship is maneuvering in the rivers or docking, an engineer is required to attend to the radio telegraph so that any commands relayed from the pilothouse to change the speed or direction of the vessel can be promptly accepted and complied with.

operation, the majority of them on the American side of the lakes, yet they account for roughly 20 percent of the total tonnage moved annually.

Industry wide, International Convention for the Prevention of Pollution from Ships (MARPOL) and federal changes (EPA) in engine emissions levels are having a large impact on vessel operators. In particular, older ships whose diesel engines burn residual fuels have a limited window of time for becoming compliant the with new standards. Many Great Lakes operators are in the process of installing new MARPOL Annex VI regulations compliant main propulsion and auxiliary diesel engines in their vessels. In addition to the cost of changing engines, the new diesels burn distillate fuel, which is considerably more expensive than the residual fuel currently in use on many ships.

The impact of these new emission regulations on the Great Lakes has yet to be fully realized. One area of major concern for American ship operators will be the application of the changes on steamships; vessels that traditionally burn residual fuel but operate with considerably lower emissions than diesel-powered vessels. The expense of upgrading these engine rooms or converting the vessels to an ATB could spell the end of active service for a number of the steamers.

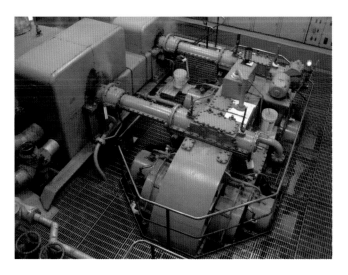

The evolution of the steam engine reached its peak in the 1950s with the marine turbine, which replaced the underpowered reciprocating engines. Turbine engines consist of two main components, a high-pressure and a low-pressure unit. The main turbine unit *Wilfred Sykes* produces 7,700 shaft horsepower at approximately 103 RPMs. The astern unit is located in the low-pressure unit. S/S *Wilfred Sykes*

The control station is the operational heart of the engine room. Nearly all engine room functions are displayed in gauges and meters on a large console. From this station, usually referred to on a steamer as the throttle deck, an engineer can monitor important functions like fuel consumption, boiler temperatures, engine and shaft RPM's, ballast conditions and electrical output.

The engine order telegraph receives engine commands from the pilothouse. In 1870 two British opticians patented their mechanical telegraph for use on ships. By 1884 over 3,000 of the telegraphs designed by C.H. and William Chadburn were installed on ships throughout the world, leading the establishment of Chadburn's (Ship) Telegraph Company Ltd. Electric telegraphs were introduced in the 1920s. The firm's engine order telegraphs were so ubiquitous that the term "Chadburn" has become synonymous with any make of standing engine order telegraph. The dial on an engine order telegraph is divided into two sections, "ahead," and "astern." Each section has 5 positions; Full, Half, Slow, Dead Slow, and Stand By. Additionally, engine order telegraph registers Stop, and Finished with Engines. S/S *American Valor*

The large brass wheels on the control console are not used for steering the ship, but for controlling the amount of steam released from the boilers to the blades in the turbines. Each steamer has a throttle for ahead and astern. Opening or closing the throttles, in essence, regulates the amount of power, or speed, requested from the pilot via the ship's radio telegraph. S/S *American Valor*

The engineers office is one of the few enclosed rooms located within the confines of the engine room. The office provides a space for technical manuals, ship's prints, parts catalogs from vendors, as well as electronic devices such as computers for ordering equipment and handling communications. S/S *American Valor*

Engineers are required to keep an engine room log for each trip. This logbook differs from the log kept in the pilothouse because it records information germane to the engine department, such as fuel consumption, miles traveled, potable water intakes, and notations from rounds made by engineers, oilers, or QMEDs. S/S *American Valor*

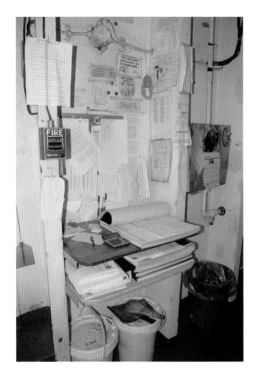

Engine rooms are multi-storied complexes with many open spaces to allow access to machinery. This view, three levels above the ship's engines, shows some of the network of catwalks, steel-grate work platforms, stairways and piping that extend both horizontally and vertically. S/S *American Valor*

Engine rooms are a catacomb of small rooms, compartments, passageways and storage areas. The old, along with the new, such as these valves, are kept handy when repairs are needed. When ships prepared for long voyages they would stow away supplies and items that could be used to repair the vessel and/or keep it in good shape given the length of a voyage between ports. The tradition remains in the maritime industry today, particularly on older ships where it is prudent to carry spare parts for emergency repairs or routine maintenance.

A small observation port on the front face of the boiler is used to visually check to ensure that there is combustion within the boiler. When a vessel is not operating at full speed, such as when they are maneuvering in the rivers or when approaching a dock, the boilers do not operate with a constant, steady load, requiring a standing watch engineer to monitor the boilers.

The era of the black-hole gangs disappeared several decades ago as coal-fired, hand-bombed ships were converted to burn fuel oil. In the conversion to burning fuel oil, boilers were automated with fuel injectors. Steamship boilers burn Bunker C fuel, also known as residual fuel. In its native state, Bunker C is a thick, heavy fuel which needs to be pre-heated before it can be used effectively to generate power.

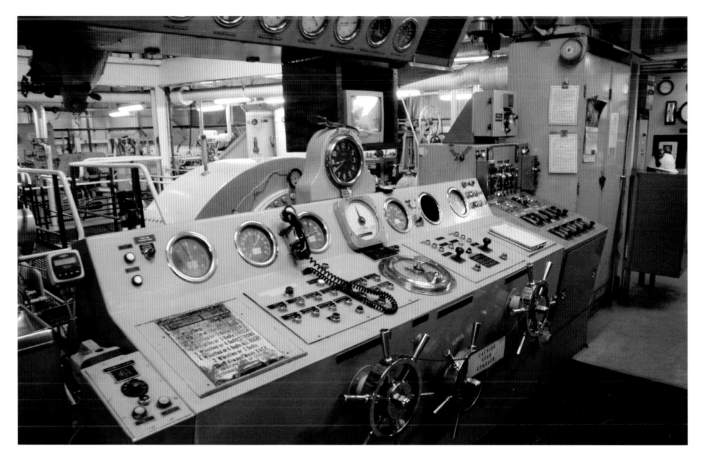

The control console sits impassively amid the daily cacophony of generators, engines, alarms and moving machinery in the engine room. In addition to the aural and visual activity, the heat generated in and around the throttle deck area can easily exceed 100 degrees. Most engineers will say they prefer the warmth of the engine room, especially when fall and winter come to the Great Lakes. S/S *Charles M. Beeghly*

Looking down on the steam turbines gives a perspective of their size. On a Great Lakes steamship most engines produce about 7,500 shaft horsepower for vessel propulsion. About one-fourth of the American Great Lakes fleet vessels are steamships. These vessels account for nearly 20 percent, just over 19 million tons, of the cargo carried annually by American vessels according to a study conducted by the U.S. Army Corps of Engineers. S/S *Charles M. Beeghly*

Most of the steamships on the Great Lakes were built before or during the 1950s. Through hull lengthening and conversion to self-unloading systems, the longevity of these vessels has been increased by several decades, helping maintain the low cost ratio of shipping via water compared to rail or truck. It is estimated that the cost of replacing one ship (the average size of those at work on the lakes in the 21st Century) would cost $70 million. S/S *Charles M. Beeghly*

At the end of the 2008 shipping season the steamer *Charles M. Beeghly* entered the shipyard at Sturgeon Bay, Wisconsin, for conversion from a steamer to a diesel-powered vessel. A sound-proofed, air-conditioned control room provides the ship's engineers with a quiet, comfortable space to monitor the machinery. The control room stands roughly where the *Beeghly's* throttle deck was situated.S/S *Charles M. Beeghly*

Two 6-cylinder B:32:40L diesels (8,040 total horsepower) were installed in the Beeghly during the engine conversion process. Rolls-Royce, a world leader in the maritime industry, produced its first marine diesel engine from Bergen, Norway, in 1943. The B32-40 diesel engine is a derivative of an engine first introduced in 1985. The B32-40 produces 500kW of power per cylinder. S/S *Charles M. Beeghly*

The diesel engines comply with new federal emissions standards set by the EPA, as well as the MARPOL Tier II standards. The Tier II standard calls for a reduction in the amount of sulfur oxide (SOx) from the current 4.5 to 3.5 percent by 2012, and down to 0.5 percent by 2020. Reductions in nitrogen oxide (NOx) are also called for in Tier II and in Tier III in 2016. Compared to trucks, the shipment of 1,000 tons of cargo by ship produces 90 percent less carbon dioxide and 70 percent less than shipment by rail.

From a compact control console located in the pilothouse, the ship's officer has complete control of the ahead and astern motion and speed of the vessel. A small joystick mounted on the console is today's modern replacement of the traditional Chadburn. The advantage here is that the navigator can react in real time to any situation encountered without having to wait for a response from the engine room. M/V *Charles M. Beeghly*

Total engine system monitoring is available within a LAN (local area network) set up on the vessel, giving the ship's officers tremendous flexibility. For instance, an engineer can monitor in real time the propulsion system, or when unloading, the mate can monitor the ballast condition of the vessel and make adjustments if needed. In the pilothouse the captain may want to monitor the amount of power being sent to the engines while maneuvering. M/V *Charles M. Beeghly*

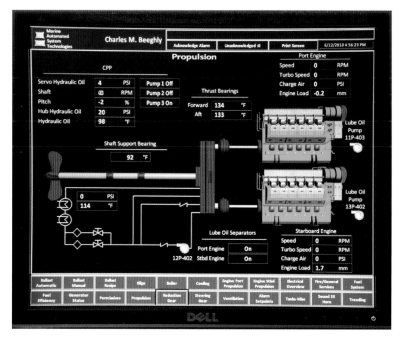

The propeller shaft extends from the engine to the after end of the ship through the stern tube where it connects with a variable pitch propeller. On the *Beeghly* the shaft turns at a constant 116 RPM. The speed of the vessel, as well as its forward or astern movement, is determined by the degree of pitch placed on the propeller. M/V *Charles M. Beeghly*

The conversion from steam to diesel has resulted in some radically different looks inside of the ship's pilothouse. In this case, a large wrap-around console was added with GPS and electronic charting monitor screens. On the right is the joystick for the vessel's main propulsion, while to the left is the control for the bow thruster. One detriment to the new design is that the console makes it difficult for the pilot to get up close to the front window to see over the bow.

In 2005 the 642-foot *Kinsman Independent* was sold and converted from steam to diesel at Hamilton, Ontario. The vessel was equipped with new General Electric V-16 diesel engines, as well as a new shaft and variable pitch propeller. The vessel is currently operating as the *Ojibway*, a member of the Lower Lakes Towing fleet. The vessel is seen here in its blue livery shortly after its conversion to diesel.

The removal of the ship's steam boilers created a large void in the engine room, leaving ample opportunity for crew members to suggest new uses for the space, such as a billiard hall or perhaps a swimming pool. The *Ojibway* is still operating in the bulk grain trade and has been fitted with a small unloading boom.

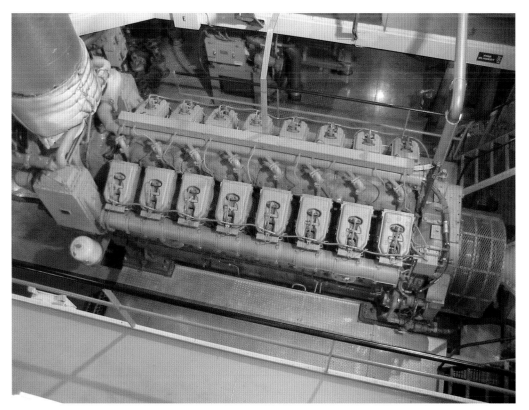

An overhead view of the *Ojibway's* 16-cylinder marine diesel engine. General Electric entered the marine diesel market in the late 1950s and is an industry leader today in the production of medium-speed marine diesel engines. This General Electric engine is a V-16, four stroke, turbo-charged 7 FDM EFI diesel engine. The engine is more compact in size, requiring a smaller footprint in the engine room. The engine weighs about 45,000 pounds overall, and is compliant with the new Tier II emissions requirements. M/V *Ojibway*

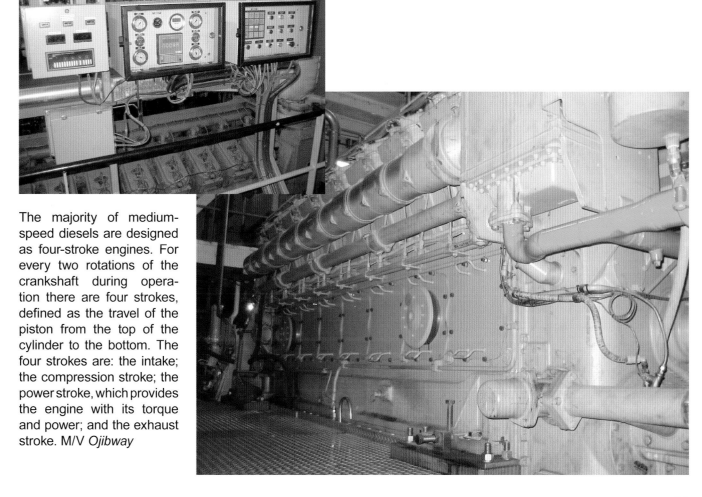

The majority of medium-speed diesels are designed as four-stroke engines. For every two rotations of the crankshaft during operation there are four strokes, defined as the travel of the piston from the top of the cylinder to the bottom. The four strokes are: the intake; the compression stroke; the power stroke, which provides the engine with its torque and power; and the exhaust stroke. M/V *Ojibway*

The ship's captain is required to be in the pilothouse when underway in connecting waterways and navigable rivers such as the St. Mary's, the St. Clair and the Detroit. In addition, a mate standing a four-hour watch is also on duty. For new mates and cadets from maritime academies, learning the rivers is a critical part for attaining licensure as a pilot. M/V *Indiana Harbor*

When it comes to the thousand-foot class of ships on the lakes the engine rooms still operate the same way; they're just bigger. Essentially, most 1,000-footers have two engine rooms, one each on the port and starboard sides. The control consoles are larger simply because there are more functions that need to be monitored. Shown here is the control console on the *Indiana Harbor*. Control levers used in the pilothouse for both the port and starboard engines, as well as the ship's bow and stern thrusters (inset), match those in the engine room and can be switched between both locations.

The 1000-foot long *Indiana Harbor*, built in 1979 at Bay Shipbuilding in Sturgeon Bay, Wisconsin, has four EMD (General Motors Electro Motive Division) engines. Each engine produces a total of 3,600 horsepower. 100 horsepower per engine is used in a reduction gear connected to the propeller shaft, so in propulsion terms, the two engines in either the port or starboard engine room produce a total of 7,000 shaft horsepower (SHP) for each shaft.

This is a view of the inboard engine on the port side of the *Indiana Harbor*. Each engine room has an inboard and outboard engine to produce the main propulsion for the ship. These engines run on No. 2 diesel fuel, except for bio-diesel fuel loaded in Minnesota ports which contains 10 percent corn oil. On a round-trip from Superior, Wisconsin, to St. Clair, Michigan, the ship will consume approximately 65,000 gallons of fuel.

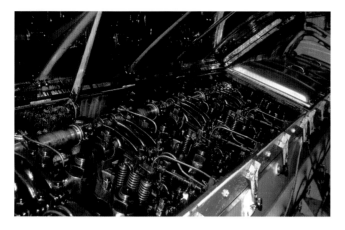

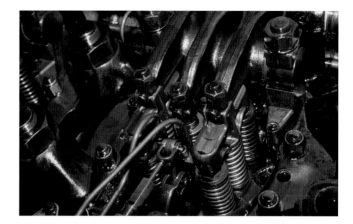

The *Indiana Harbor*'s EMD series 645-E7 engines are two-stroke, 20-cylinder engines. Each cylinder (inset) has a displacement of 645 cubic inches and a stroke of 10 inches (254 mm), with a bore of nine and one-sixteenth inches (230.2 mm), at a compression ratio of 14.5. The cylinder is the space in which the piston travels and is typically made of cast aluminum or iron. The turbocharged EMD engines on the *Indiana Harbor* were designed to produce 2.7 MW of power per engine.

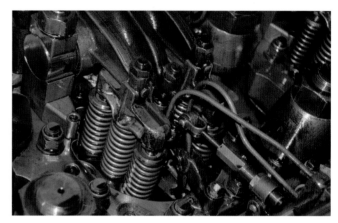

The Danish firm Burmeister and Wain have been producing diesel engines since Rudolf Diesel first granted the firm exclusive rights to manufacture his invention in 1899. The first diesel-powered ocean going vessel, the M/S *Selandia*, sailed in 1912, ushering in an era that would forever change navigation on the high seas. A number of vessels registered on the Canadian side of the Great Lakes are equipped with Burmeister and Wain diesel engines, such as the one on the ULS Group vessel *John D. Leitch*. One of the many characteristics of this 7,000 horsepower engine is its immense size. From the engine foundation to the cylinder heads (inset), the engine extends upwards of three deck levels. Burmeister & Wain engines continue powering many ships around the world. M/V *John D. Leitch*

Engineers on the *J. W. Shelley* take advantage of a couple days in port to change a damaged cylinder liner (right). The *Shelley* is powered by four 2-stroke cycle, 12-cylinder Fairbanks-Morse diesel engines; all total, that's 96 vertically opposed pistons. The engines on the *Shelley* burn marine diesel fuel, also known as distillate. For diesel-powered ships there are two main types of fuel: distillate and residual. Distillate is the by-product of the distillation process of boiling crude. Intermediate fuels are created in the distillation process by regulating the amount of gas oil that is left in the non-boiling fractions. Intermediate fuel can also be created by blending with distillate fuel. Often ships will burn distillate when maneuvering and then switch over to the cheaper residual fuel when underway.

One of the sixteen ballast pumps and motors on the ship *Indiana Harbor*. There are eight on each side of the vessel. The pump is in the foreground; the taller unit behind it is the motor.

Besides providing power to the ship for propulsion and daily operation, taking on or pumping out ballast is one of the most important functions performed by the staff of the ship's engine room. Ballast is any material heavy enough to stabilize the ship; in most cases this means cargo or water. Ballast water is pumped out when the ship is loading and subsequently taken in during the unloading of the vessel. Ballast water from the tanks is pumped out the side of the ship through large pipes (below) located on the lower level of the engine room. At maximum capacity, the ballast can be pumped at 40,000 gallons per minute. M/V *Indiana Harbor*

Ballast water being discharged out the port side of the *Indiana Harbor*.

To comply with regulations for the control of invasive species on the Great Lakes, all ships, whether domestic or foreign, are required to submit a Ballast Water Reporting Form for each voyage. Included in the report are the locations (latitude and longitude) for the intake source and discharge location of the ballast, the volume of water stored, and the tanks where it is stored. M/V *Indiana Harbor*

On the *Indiana Harbor*, ballast water is monitored in the engine department's control room. A data display screen shows the water volume in each of the ship's ballast tanks. Digital ballast readouts are relatively new to the shipping industry. For many years king gauges, half-inch diameter glass tube columns filled with mercury, were the standard method for monitoring ballast water conditions in the engine room or from the pilot house. Health concerns about the possibility of direct exposure to the mercury have led to its removal from most vessels.

Another vital function of the engine department is to produce electricity for the ship. Throughout the season the ship is self-reliant for all of its electrical needs. Power is generated with the use of multiple, mid-sized generators. In 2010, two new, state-of-the-art diesel generators were installed on the *Indiana Harbor*. These new generators utilize Caterpillar's ACERT technology which features multiple fuel injection, specialized electronic controllers, refined air management technology and advanced combustion design to meet current and future EPA emission standards. The port and starboard generators produce 600 kW of power (60,000 watts) for use on the *Indiana Harbor* during all phases of operation, including peak usage during unloading cycles. The electrical station on the *Indiana Harbor* is located inside the control room where it can be easily accessed by the ship's engineers. The new EPA guidelines are being phased in on the Great Lakes with the goal of ultimately reducing particulate matter (PM) emissions from these engines by as much as 90 percent and NOx (nitrogen oxides) emissions by as much as 80 percent when fully implemented.

Shipboard electrical station.

Control panel for Caterpillar diesel engines.

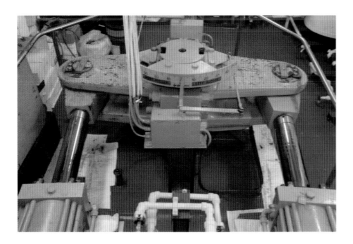

With thousands of horsepower, pushing a ship up to three football fields long, that is loaded with a cargo of over 60,000 tons of iron ore, you might wonder how easy it is to turn a ship that large? It's not like the image you see in the movies of an old sailing ship with several men holding onto the wheel in a storm-tossed sea. Steering systems today operate in tandem with the ship's wheel in the pilothouse and turn the ship in two directions, to port or to starboard. The steering system is connected to the ship's rudder and is typically powered by an electric motor. When the wheelsman makes a course adjustment a signal is sent to the steering system via a hydraulic or electric telemotor. On ships with two engine rooms there is a steering system for each propeller shaft. The steering system at the after end of the *Charles M. Beeghly* (below) is typical of systems in use on single shaft Great Lakes vessels.

Most ship engines have a higher rotational speed than the propeller shaft needs so a reduction gear is used to reduce the speed of the shaft. This reduction gear on the *Indiana Harbor* reduces the 3,600 horsepower engines by 100 horsepower to a shaft horsepower of 3,500 per engine. On steamers, the high and low pressure turbines each have their own crankshafts that are run through a double reduction gearbox.

Shafts are usually made of high tensile brass or aluminum bronze. Metal alloys are favored because of their non-corrosive properties. Propeller shafts are held in place and alignment with a series of bearings that support the shaft between the thrust block and the stern tube.

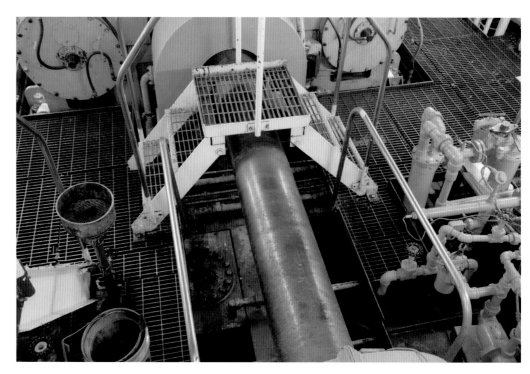

The third main component in a ship's propulsion system is its propulsor. The screw propeller, seen here on the *Mississagi*, is a typical propulsor found on many Great Lakes ships. On this style of propeller, known as a built-up propeller, the individual blades or "buckets" are removable. Ice conditions on the lakes during spring and winter months can cause damage to the blades, so being able to easily change a damaged blade without an expensive trip to a shipyard is one of the main advantages to using this kind of propeller. Extra blades are usually produced for a particular propeller for this purpose and are carried on board the ship in the event of any damage.

Spare propeller blade on the stern of the *American Spirit*.

Seeing a person standing next to one of the propeller blades on a thousand-foot ship gives a sense of the immense size of these ships. An individual blade of this propeller on *Indiana Harbor* is about the size of a grown man.

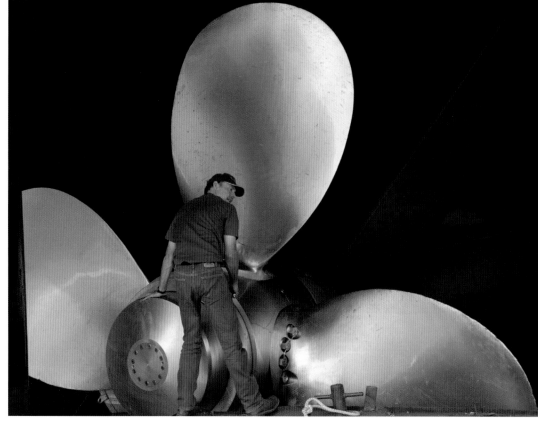

Stopping a 30,000- to 60,000-ton ship is not as simple as stepping on the brakes. Ships don't have brakes, but they do have anchors which serve to stop the vessel, keep the vessel in one place, or to assist in slowing or turning the vessel when maneuvering. While it is not common for ships on the Great Lakes to carry a spare anchor because they are close enough to a port should they lose one, ships that work on both the lakes and the ocean often carry a spare anchor. The spare anchor secured to the fo'csle deck of the *Atlantic Erie* is known as a Baldt type stockless anchor.

Anchors are secured to the ship with anchor chain that is fed through the hawse pipe. The flukes on the Baldt anchor are designed for catching on nearly all underwater surfaces. Upon retrieval, the anchor sometimes needs to be cleaned of mud and debris. Ship anchors weigh about 12,000 pounds each.

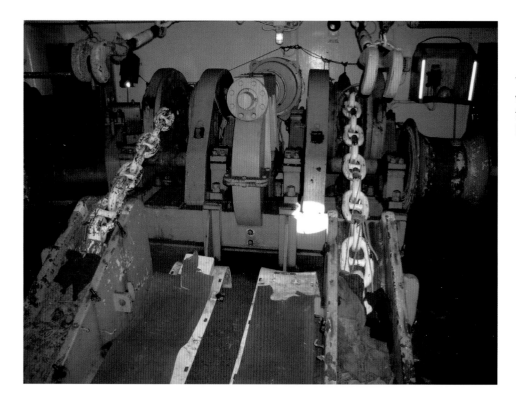

The wildcat is a sprocketed wheel that engages the links of the anchor chain to pay out or haul in the anchor chain.

The large yellow hook, called the devil's claw, is used as an emergency safety stopper if the chain jumps off the wildcat.

When a ship is underway the anchor chains are secured to prevent them from accidentally falling.

Close-up view of the anchor chain as it enters the riding chock. The chock prevents the chain from fouling on the deck.

Great Lakes freighters carry three anchors: two on the bow, one to port and the other to starboard, and a stern anchor. The anchors are held in place and released with an electric-powered anchor windlass. On nearly all vessels the forward windlass is in an enclosed area, often called the windlass room, on the spar deck level. The stern windlass is usually located outside on the fantail of the ship. On older ships, such as the *Lee A. Tregurtha*, the anchor windlass is located outside. The anchors are secured to the windlass with 2.5-inch steel chain. Each ship is required to carry at minimum the length of the ship in anchor chain for the bow anchors, and half the ship's length in chain for the stern anchor.

A nine month shipping season means that the ships have to work virtually non-stop to move all of the tonnage contracted to them each season. It's a twenty-four hour, seven days a week job. When something breaks down it needs to be fixed, often immediately. The engineering department not only needs to keep the ship's engines running, but they are also responsible for literally every functioning item on the ship. From dishwashers to toilets, electrical fixtures to diesel engines, the ship's engineer is a jack-of-all-trades.

Deck winches get a lot of use and are exposed to all of the elements. Keeping the deck machinery operating is a regular part of the engine departments work load. M/V *Indiana Harbor*

Engineers are often thought of as the denizens of the deep, but taking advantage of being able to work outside on a nice day isn't something to be missed. M/V *Maritime Trader*

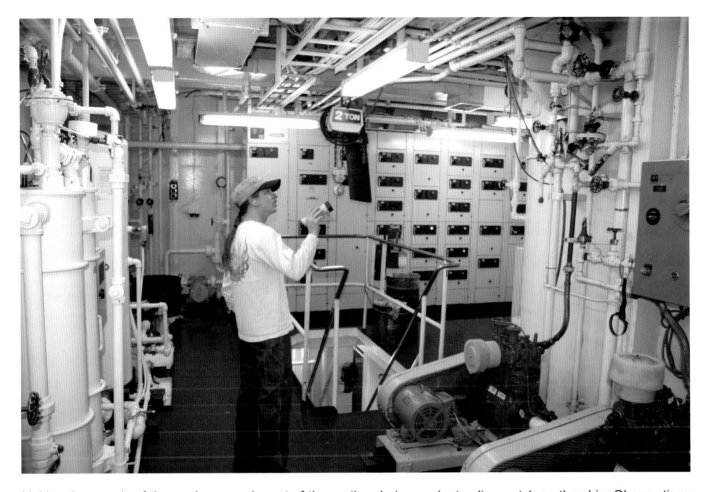

Making the rounds of the engine room is part of the routine during each standing watch on the ship. Observations and notes are made by junior engineers and reported back to the First Engineer or Chief so that action can be taken if necessary. M/V *American Republic*

A new spray system is added to the end of the unloading boom. Water and/or chemicals are sprayed onto commodities during discharge as fire retardants or for dust control. S/S *Kaye E. Barker*

CHAPTER 3:
The Captain's Toolbox: Navigation

Navigation of the vessel is the domain of the captain and officers of the ship's deck department. Ships on the Great Lakes operate on a 24/7 schedule. Within those 24-hour periods ship life is divided into work segments called "watches." There are three watches per 24 hours; the 12-to-4 watch, usually the domain of the 3rd Mate; the 4-to-8 watch, the 1st Mate's watch; and the 8-to-12 for the 2nd Mate. For each pilothouse watch there is also a wheelsman to steer the ship.

When the ship is underway the Mates are responsible for setting the correct course to the next destination, giving the orders to the wheelsman to steer that course, and for updating the ship's position on the navigation chart during their four-hour watch. When the vessel is in an area of restricted navigation most companies require the captain to be present in the pilothouse. Restricted waters on the Great Lakes include the St. Mary's River above and below the Soo Locks, the St. Clair and Detroit rivers, the two major connecting arteries between Huron and Erie known collectively as "the rivers," and the Welland Canal, as well as all harbors and smaller rivers. In all instances, unless someone is training to become a relief captain, the captain takes the ship into and out of all docks and harbors. The ship's mates assist the captain from various stations on the deck, acting as an additional pair of eyes to provide information about the ship's position. This ship handling is the part of the job that all captains relish.

The safety of the ship and its crew is paramount. A number of electronic aids are available to assist the crew in the safe navigation of the vessel. At least two radar units, either an X-band or S-band, are required in the pilothouse. Many ships have a third unit, usually an older one, as an additional back-up. Radar is used to see surrounding objects at a distance beyond the pilot's eyesight, especially at night and during inclement weather. Pilotage regulations for ships operating on the St. Lawrence Seaway require at least one short-range (X-band) and one long-range (S-band) radar unit.

Electronic charting is another aid to navigation that has become a part of everyday ship operation. The electronic charts mirror the ship's paper charts, although the paper charts are still considered the official reference for navigation. What the captains like about the electronic charting is the ability to customize the chart with their local knowledge of conditions, in harbors or for approaches to docks. Repeater stations in the captain's office, and other places on the ship, allow the captains to monitor the ship's position when they are not in the pilothouse.

Knowing the ship's position at any given time is not just important to the captain, but also to governmental and regulatory bodies that track the overall integrity of the Great Lakes and St. Lawrence Seaway System. The use of AIS, Automated Identification System, is required by the U.S. Coast Guard and by law is required to be programmed with the correct information. An AIS display shows information about other ships in the vicinity, their closest point of approach, heading and destination, and cargo on board.

Vessels using AIS have fewer check-in points with the Coast Guard regulated traffic departments such as Soo Traffic, Sarnia Traffic, and the various control stations on the St. Lawrence Seaway. Traffic within these waterways is monitored for speed and weather conditions during the regular shipping season. During winter navigation the ship traffic is controlled by the Coast Guard cutters working in each area.

More traditional navigation aids such as range lights, lighthouses, and navigation and weather buoys are in place throughout the Great Lakes, although seasonal changes may take some of them out of service for several months of the season.

Navigational aids are there to assist the ship's officers in their decision making. The ship's officers still have to be able to interpret the information they are receiving and make qualified evaluations to keep the ship from harm. For the captain and his officers, electronics are the wrenches and screwdrivers in the toolbox. Choosing which one to use in any given situation can only be done based on years of training and experience.

There's something magical about watching a ship as it glides past, and in nearly all instances the pilothouse is the focal point of attention. Mark Twain immortalized river pilots in his vivid stories of the Mississippi River in such a way that the pilot house of nearly any ship afloat has an aura of Americana to it. The Great Lakes steamer *Edward L. Ryerson* is one of the most ardently admired vessels of all time.

They are called the "brain box" by some...the ultimate separation of church and state on the water, or better put—the deck department vs. the engine department. When iron and steel ships took to the lakes the pilots, wheelsman, look-outs, and watchmen were all assembled together at the forward end of the ship. Save for the vision of Alexander MacDougall's whalebacks, it stayed that way for the better part of a century. M/V *Algorail*

The 1970s brought the evolution of ship design to a utilitarian evenhandedness, bundling ten to twelve stories of engine room, berthing accommodations, galley and utility rooms and the navigational level into one large block at the after end of the ship. Purists decried it, but the deck crews that had to walk back aft for meals in foul weather, if they could, easily bade farewell to the old days. Modern integrated ship management begins with one homogenous crew. M/V *Indiana Harbor*

A late night foray into a thunderstorm paints the pilot-house of the *Paul R. Tregurtha* in a smear of color against a somber lake and sky. The *Paul R. Tregurtha* is the largest vessel on the Great Lakes at 1,013 feet in length. The vessel works heavily in the low sulfur coal trade from Superior, Wisconsin, to power stations on the St. Clair River, near Detroit, and on Lake Erie. When on the open lake the pilothouse is manned by an officer, or mate, and a wheelsman.

On ships where the pilothouse is placed at the forward end of the vessel the captain has a commanding view of the water in front of the ship. The area front and center ahead of the wheel stand is the domain of the captain or the ship's mates. From this position they give steering commands to the wheelsman, and monitor the array of navigational and weather instruments in the pilothouse. M/V *Canadian Miner*

Visibility is of utmost importance for safe navigation of the vessel. The pilothouse, whether it is located at the forward end or the after end of the ship, is designed to provide pilots with a 360-degree view of the vessel. Large expanses of glass stretch nearly 100 feet from port to starboard on the thousand-footers giving the captain the ability to look down the side of the ship when it is alongside the dock.

The ship's captain is responsible for the navigation of the vessel. It is the captain's job to bring the ship into a dock, to depart the dock, and to be on duty during the river portions of each trip. Here the captain guides his 1,000-foot vessel toward the Poe Lock at Sault Ste. Marie. It takes many years to attain the rank of captain. For many "old school" mariners this meant working their way up from entry-level deck work to wheelsman and then mate. M/V *Indiana Harbor*

The graceful arc of windows inside of a classically styled laker. For Canadian captains running the Seaway grain trade, having the front window view is helpful in keeping an eye on all the activity that goes on when transiting the system locks. For a ship down-bound to Lake Ontario, the Welland Canal has eight locks to pass through. Once clear of Lake Ontario there are an additional seven locks along the Seaway. M/V *Maritime Trader*

Updating the navigation charts is the responsibility of the ship's 2nd Mate. Changes to charts occur frequently and are issued by the United States Coast Guard. Changes to charts are usually cut out and pasted into place (right) until the chart is worn out and replaced.

The chart table is a fixture found in all pilot houses. In many instances, such as on the *Indiana Harbor*, it is located in a separate room so a light can be used if needed at night. Ships are required to carry up-to-date charts for all areas where they may possibly navigate. The chart table is usually where the ship's navigational log is kept for each voyage and is also used as a working space to record navigational notes and repair orders.

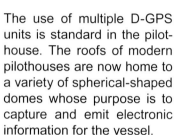

The use of multiple D-GPS units is standard in the pilothouse. The roofs of modern pilothouses are now home to a variety of spherical-shaped domes whose purpose is to capture and emit electronic information for the vessel.

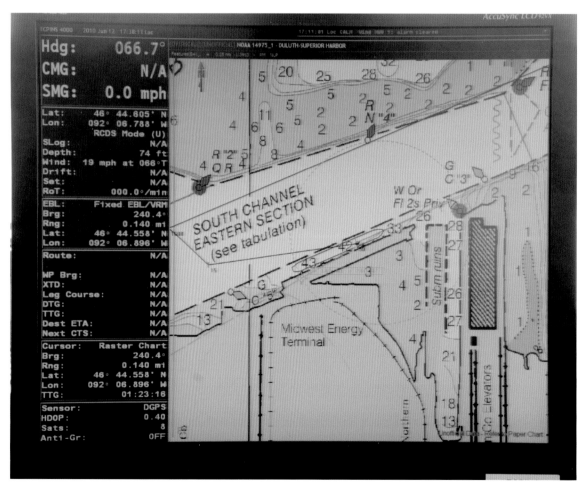

The advent of electronic charting has had a major impact on shipboard navigation. Captains are now able to set up routes into well frequented docks and harbors that take advantage of their specific knowledge as well as that of the traditional chart. Electronic charts first came on line in the mid 1990s, but any good captain will tell that it is still only one of several tools available for use.

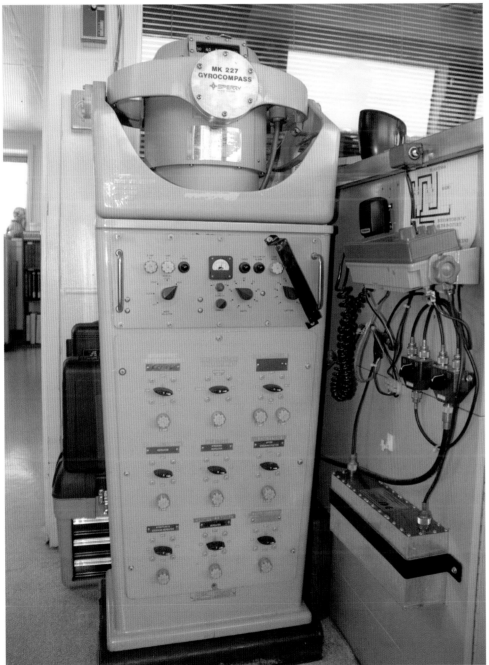

The gyro compass is the ship's primary tool for determining its exact position at any given time. The gyro is not affected by magnetic anomalies or interference, such as the steel hull or cabins of the ship, therefore it is able to indicate true north without any deviations. All Great Lakes vessels have a gyro compass with automated repeaters at the wheelstand, in the engine room, and often in the captain's office. The gyro compass was developed in 1908 by Elmer Sperry. By World War I his compass was in use by the U.S. Navy. The MK-227 Sperry gyrocompass in use here is on the 1,000-footer *Indiana Harbor*, operated by the American Steamship Company.

As technology advances, more ship-board electronics are going digital, including the gyrocompass. The latest advance for Sperry is the Navgat X MX 2 gyrocompass and its companion Navpilot 4000 steering stand. The digital gyrocompass installed in 2009 on the *Charles M. Beeghly* is located several decks below the pilothouse. The positional information is relayed from the main gyrocompass to multiple repeaters within the ship, including the wheelstand in the pilothouse.

Sailing in fog or limited visibility due to rain or snow is a tangible factor to Great Lakes navigators. M/V *Charles M. Beeghly*

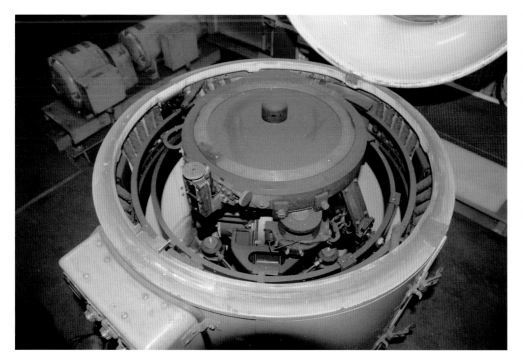

The gyrocompass, based on the concept of a gyro, is suspended by gimbals inside the unit so that it floats independently of the ship's movement. This gyrocompass on the *Charles M. Beeghly* was installed in 1959 when the ship was completed as the *Shenango II*. This old Sperry unit has not been in service for quite a few years.

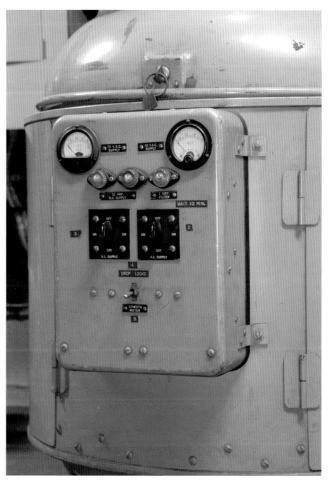

As upgrades are installed, these older gyrocompass units are often left on the ship. Because of their canister design they are sometimes referred to as vacuum cleaners, or using a more contemporary reference as "R2's," the units being comparable in size and shape to the Star Wars droid unit. The gyrocompasses were powered with an electric motor and usually were housed in an electrical locker in the forward end of the ship.

Original wooden and replacement wheel on the Steamer *Edward L. Ryerson.*

The large iron wheel on the 1940s-era motor vessel *Manistee.*

Unlike your passenger car or SUV's steering wheel, which tend to come in rather uniform sizes, a ship's steering wheel can vary greatly in size, and in composition. Some are made of wood, some shaped from iron, and now many are made of a high-grade plastic. Their size will also vary, from small to large. The ship's wheelstand is usually mounted on a platform to allow the wheelsman to see over the head of the pilot in front of them. This stand on the M/V *Edgar B. Speer* shows the magnetic compass, the wheelstand with gyrocompass repeater, and the engine-order telegraph.

Emergency steering stations: (left) *Joseph Frantz*, (right) *Manistee*, (below) *Indiana Harbor.*

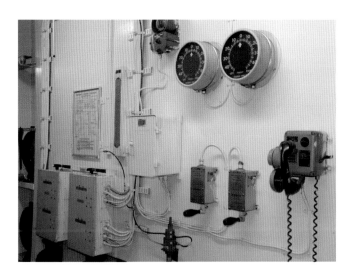

If the ship loses power and the electronic steering fails, it's back to the basics with the use of the ship's backup emergency steering station. On the older steamships the station is typically positioned outdoors on the after boat deck. On ships built after 1970 the station is located in the ship's engine room. The emergency station consists of a wheel or lever, a compass and either a wireless radio or a magneto phone system for communication.

Ships working on the Great Lakes rarely go more than twenty-four hours without being in some kind of restrictive waterway, whether it is a lock, a connecting channel or a river. In these confined areas a loss of steering could cause the ship to run aground or strike another vessel. Here, a thousand-footer enters the narrow Neebish Channel in the St. Marys River.

The Furuno FAR2827 X-Band radar console is one of three radar units on the bridge of the *Charles M. Beeghly*.

All commercial vessels have a minimum of two main radars, plus an additional back-up unit. Ships of the Interlake Steamship Company utilize short and long range Furuno radar units. Radar units are classified by their transmission frequency. For commercial usage, vessels operate an X-band (3cm frequency) for short range detection, and an S-band (10cm frequency) for long range. The six-foot wide X-band antenna is mounted on the top of the pilothouse. M/V *Charles M. Beeghly*

Radar screens display two types of resolution, range and bearing, giving the operator the ability to distinguish objects that are in close proximity to each other. In bearing resolution, the narrower the horizontal beam the higher the resolution. Range resolution is determined by the length of the radar's pulse. A shorter the pulse length equates to finer object resolution.

The Furuno S-Band radar unit on the bridge of the *Charles M. Beeghly*. Many veteran captains can recall their early years as a ship's mate when they were only allowed to turn on the radar unit, but never use it. Today, all mates are required to understand and utilize radar. The S-band is considered a long-range-radar and has excellent ability to see targets through heavy weather. Radars emit radio pulses which travel at 186,000 miles per second. The pulses hit their target and return at the same constant speed, thereby relaying almost instantaneous information. The antenna, also known as a scanner unit, is mounted on the highest possible place on ship to achieve maximum detection range. The S-band antenna is 9 feet in width and rotates 360 degrees as it emits narrow RF beams. The narrower the beam, the sharper the image.

The pilothouse of the 806-foot long laker *Charles M. Beeghly.*

The forward mast and 9-foot Furuno antenna atop the *Beeghly's* pilothouse.

Darkness has settled in on the 8-to-12 watch aboard the *Indiana Harbor.* Rain pelts the ship as it moves steadily down the Saginaw Bay toward Detroit Edison's Essexville power plant. In addition to both the short and long-range radars, was well as the ship's electronic charting (ECPINs), the captain also uses the ship's xenon arc searchlights to find the navigation buoys in the narrow channel.

The use of electronic charting systems (ECDIS) came into use in the early 1990s. Pioneered by the Canadian firm Offshore Systems in the 1970s, the use of its computerized navigation technology hit the Great Lakes in 1993 when Canada Steamship Lines installed the ECPIN (Electronic Chart Precise Integrated Navigation System) units on all of its vessels. ECPIN units are in use on nearly all Great Lakes freighters as another pilothouse tool for navigation.

The anemometer atop the pilothouse relays wind velocity to a digital monitor in the pilothouse.

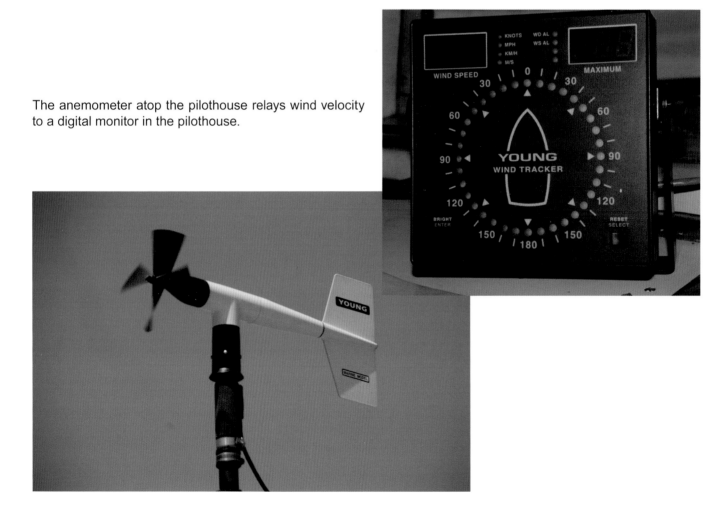

The nine-foot blade of the *Indiana Harbor*'s long-range radar on stand-by.

If you think your neighborhood roofs are cluttered with satellite dishes and television aerials, then the rooftop of a modern ship is going to seem like a major communications center, which it is. Traditional devices, such as radar antenna and navigation lights and buggy-whip radio aerials are now being closed in upon by numerous mushroom and dome-shaped transmitters and receivers handling everything from global positioning information to satellite communication and television.

CHAPTER 4:
Ships at Work: Trip Cycle—Loading

At any given time there are hundreds of ships at work on the Great Lakes. How do these ships work? What goes on when they are in port, loading, unloading, or when they are underway? This is the heart of the story...of how ships on the Great Lakes work. The best way to explain is to walk through a typical trip cycle for a ship.

The ship's official log-books record each load through unload cycle as a "trip." Larger ships, like thousand-footers, will make fewer trips during the season because they carry more tonnage per trip than a smaller ship. For a large ship one trip may take 3 to 5 days to complete. A smaller vessel working in the stone trade may make as many as 3 trips in a single day, and over a hundred during the entire season.

The start of a trip usually begins after the cargo has been discharged and the ship heads to its next loading destination. The first part of the cycle follows the activity on board from the arrival at the dock, through the loading process.

The *American Republic* (above) began its trip to Silver Bay in the protected waters of Green Bay where it unloaded a cargo of coal. A day and a half later the ship arrives at Silver Bay to load iron ore for Cleveland. Most ships will back into the dock at Silver Bay, turning outside the harbor basin before backing down to the dock. The extremely maneuverable *Republic*, with four propellers and eight rudders, marks its arrival with an impressive 360-degree turn inside the basin.

The number of cargoes hauled by a ship working on the Great Lakes is kept on record in the ship's logbook. Some ships make as many as 130 trips a season while others average around 50. For some fleets a trip begins with the loading of a cargo, for others it begins with the unloading—either way, a trip is considered one cycle of load and unload on the lakes. The *American Spirit* makes its way into the Superior harbor.

The bottom line is not how many trips each ship will make in the season, but how much tonnage they will carry, and how safely they will accomplish the job. The Great Lakes shipping industry has one of the highest safety records of any industry while often working in extreme environmental conditions and at a variety of industrial sites. The *Joseph L. Block* is seen here arriving at Carmeuse's Cedarville dock to load dolomite, part of a split cargo begun at Port Inland.

A half century ago nearly every ship on the Great Lakes arriving at a dock required the assistance of a harbor tug. For any ship going up a river, such as the Cuyahoga or the Rouge, it was a given that at least one, and often two tugs, were needed. All of that changed in the early 1960s with the introduction of the bow thruster. In the late 1970s stern thrusters were being added to save cost and time. M/V *Peter Cresswell*

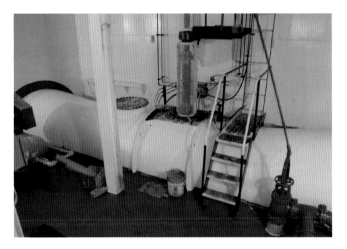

A bow thruster is basically a large tube placed through the hull of the ship between the collision bulkhead and the stem. On most ships it is almost impossible to get a look at the thruster tunnel, but on the barge *Pathfinder* the tunnel is easily accessible. To the left of the walkway is the motor that drives the propeller inside the tube. There is an access hatch on top of the tube to the left of the motor.

Bow and stern thrusters are powered by small diesel engines of 500 to 1,000 horsepower, like the one here on the steamer *American Valor*. The bow thruster operates by pushing water to the port or starboard side of the ship, giving the captain the control needed to move the ship toward or away from a dock.

A roiling torrent of water surges between the ship and the dock as the *Maritime Trader* approaches the dock at the Bunge Elevator at Quebec City.

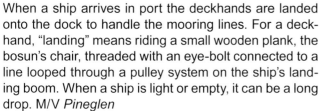

When a ship arrives in port the deckhands are landed onto the dock to handle the mooring lines. For a deckhand, "landing" means riding a small wooden plank, the bosun's chair, threaded with an eye-bolt connected to a line looped through a pulley system on the ship's landing boom. When a ship is light or empty, it can be a long drop. M/V *Pineglen*

Once the deckhands are on the dock, heaving lines are used to pull the steel mooring lines from the ship to bollards located along the dock. The *Gordon C. Leitch* has just arrived at Duluth's CN ore dock, which has just been washed free of pellets.

While many docks are frequently used and are kept clean of debris and obstructions there are always exceptions, especially in small ports where less than a handful of ships are seen every year. In these instances it is not unusual to have deckhands walking on rotten timbers, piles of taconite, stone or coal, or wading through brush and weeds. Add rain or snow and night to this mix and it can easily become a dangerous situation. M/V *American Republic*

Lightweight heaving lines are used to pull the heavier steel mooring cables from the ship to the dock. If the ship is loaded too deep for the water draft of the dock, it may take several deckhands to pull the heavy cables to the dock. There is always the potential of being pulled into the water when working on the edge of a dock, so wearing lifejackets is a mandatory safety requirement. S/S *Kaye E. Barker*

The mate manning the mooring winch directs the deckhands in the placement of the cables on the dock. If the vessel will need to shift up and down the dock while loading, lines are set to warp the ship along the dock. M/V *Indiana Harbor*

A mooring winch is the device used to pay out or haul in the steel cables, or "wires" used to berth or tie-up the ship to a dock. The barrel, or drum, is where the cable is wrapped to the winch. Most winches are driven by a 50 horsepower direct-current motor. Most ships have four to six deck winches for mooring the vessel. ATB *Pathfinder*

The mooring lines are threaded through chalks mounted on the side of the ship. Mooring systems are self-tensioning so that the lines remain taut as the ship settles while loading, or pay out cable when the ship rises in the water during unloading. Electric drive controls are mounted along the side of the ship near the chalks so the winch operator can see along the dock while controlling the cable. M/V *CSL Assiniboine*

Looking over the top of winch drum. When the ship is tied to the dock two winches are used at the aft end of the spar deck and two are used at the forward end of the spar deck. Additional lines can be set from the fo'csle or the fantail if needed. A standard mooring wire is made of 1-inch diameter plowed steel, and is between 500 to 650 feet in length. S/S *Kaye E. Barker*

A deckhand stands shrouded in a veil of steam while working with a steam-powered hatch winch. In the days before the one-piece hatch covers, telescoping hatch covers were pulled open or shut with the use of a steam winch. Superheated steam used to power the ship's engines was sent through pressure reducing valves so that it could be used on deck. On deck winches and windlasses the steam engine was slowly warmed with all the steam drains open to build up pressure. While in operation, steam returns send condensed steam back to the engine room where it is eventually returned into the boiler feed system (diesel powered main engine but winches were steam driven). M/V *Joseph Frantz*

Prior to the introduction of diesel-powered engines and electric motors, steam was used to power nearly everything on the ship. On the inside, steam heated rooms, provided hot water for showers and for the galley's steam tables, while on deck the steam powered anchor windlasses, mooring winches and hatch winches.

For the deckhand the hatch crane is probably the greatest back-saving invention to come along for the deck, next to single-piece hatch covers. A century ago, hatch covers were made of wood and took multiple sections to cover a hatch, all of which required two men to manually lift them off and later, back over the hatch. The wooden hatches were later replaced with leaf, or telescoping hatch covers. These were pulled over the hatch with the assistance of a steel cable powered by a steam winch. Telescoping hatches were equally back-breaking and dangerous for fingers and hands unexpectedly caught in the leaf. The development of the single-piece hatch and a crane to lift the hatch has greatly reduced injury.

Once the vessel is secured at the dock the hatch covers are removed in preparation for loading. Most ships have between 20 to 23 hatch covers that need to be removed. Thousand-footers have 37 hatch covers. The hatch covers are lifted with a deck crane that travels the length of the deck on rails. Most single-piece hatches are 11 feet wide by 44 feet long and are spaced 24 feet to center.

A look down the deck of the 1,000-foot ore carrier *Edgar B. Speer* shows the open hatches as the ship gets ready to load. Because the *Speer* was built to haul only iron ore, a cargo that is dense in proportion to its cubic capacity, the hatch openings are smaller than most ships. In the case of the *Speer*, and other ships like its fleet-mate the *Edwin H. Gott*, the iron ore is loaded in the center of a sloped cargo hold and does not fill all the way out to the side or the top of the cargo hold.

The *Gordon C. Leitch* has perhaps the most unique hatch covers of any ship on the lakes. The vessel was built as a self-unloader by means of a moveable deck rig that proved ineffective for use on the lakes and was subsequently removed. The hatches, at an unusual 14.02m x 28.35m, and their odd-sized covers, remained.

Single-piece hatch covers fade to infinity on the large ships. A typical hatch cover weighs upwards of half-dozen tons, and can, depending upon the size of the hatch cover, have around a hundred hatch clamps. The hatch coaming is the raised frame that supports the hatch cover. Coamings are usually about one to two feet high and help prevent water from entering the cargo hold.

A look down the spar deck of a working laker shows why the deck hands refer to this as the hatch farm. During loading and unloading the hatch covers need to be unclamped and removed, only to be re-set and re-clamped when the work is done. On older ships with only a one-foot clearance between hatches, bruised and bloodied shins were among the common maladies of the deck hand. M/V *CSL Tadoussac*

The steeply sloped cargo hold on the *American Integrity* is designed to allow the cargo to easily slide down into the gate opening at the bottom of the hold for discharge onto the conveyor system.

The cargo hold on the *CSL Assiniboine* is not sloped, which allows the vessel to carry cargos such as coal, limestone, grain or other bulk commodities. On this ship front-end loaders are used to shove cargo onto the belt.

Self-unloading technology came of age on the Great Lakes in the 1970s. All new construction, both American and Canadian, featured self-unloading systems. Older ships, most of these American ships operating in the ore and coal trades, were converted to self-unloaders. Some ships, like the *Algosteel*, have two belts that merge the cargo at the elevator or loop-belt end. One advantage of the two-belt system is the ability to easily blend cargoes, such as dolomite and hi-cal limestone.

Once the ship is secured to the dock the boarding ladder is set. Placement of the ladder is dependent upon the dock and the proximity of the after or forward end of the ship to access points at the dock. Some ships use a gangway that is secured at mid-ship. The gangway, or accommodation ladder, is a stepped ramp positioned at a less severe incline than the boarding ladder. Using a boarding ladder on an empty ship, particularly on a thousand-footer that has a deeper cargo hold, can mean an ascent of up to fifty feet. In the new era of post-911 Homeland Security, ships are required to maintain only one access point and to keep the ladder lifted off the dock to prevent unauthorized boarding of the vessel.

Security is an important aspect of today's merchant shipping industry. All vessels are required to maintain records of every arrival and departure from the vessel. This includes crew, maintenance personnel, dock workers, family, friends, and company employees. While in port the wheelsman on watch is responsible to keep the ship's security log. Homeland Security regulations require that all expected visitors to the ship be listed on the ship's roster 24 hours prior to arriving in port.

Iron ore continues to be the largest cargo by tonnage shipped on the Great Lakes. Iron ore shipped from Michigan ports, such as Escanaba, accounted for over 12 million tons in 2008. Ore shipped at Escanaba and Marquette comes primarily from the Tilden and Empire mines of Michigan's Marquette Iron Range and from the Minorca mine at Virginia, Minnesota. S/S *Kaye E. Barker*

Minnesota ports account for the largest volume of iron ore moved on the Great Lakes, due to their proximity to the massive Mesabi Iron Range. The first ore shipped from the port of Two Harbors was loaded in 1884. Over a hundred years later, Two Harbors remains a vital link in the Lake Superior to lower lakes iron ore trade. The Canadian laker *Gordon C. Leitch* loads for Hamilton, Ontario. Canada is the world's largest foreign importer of Great Lakes iron ore, receiving between 8 to 10 million tons annually.

Wisconsin's lone ore port of Superior ships between 10 to 12 million tons per year. Pellets arrive at the Burlington-Northern Santa Fe Railroad dock from Hibbing Taconite and Keewatin Taconite to be loaded onto ships bound for the steel mills of lower Lake Michigan. The *Stewart J. Cort*, loading here at Superior's BNSF Dock 5, runs virtually non-stop all season carrying Hibbing pellets between Superior to ArcelorMittal's steel mill at Burns Harbor, Indiana.

Iron ore pellets pour from one of the loading shuttles at Duluth's Canadian National ore dock into the thousand-foot vessel *American Spirit*. Pellets arrive at Duluth twice daily in 140-car unit trains from the United Taconite plant at Forbes, Minnesota. The Duluth dock has a 3 million ton ground storage capacity. Three reclaimers feed a 48-inch conveyor that carries the ore to the 20 shiploading bins and shuttles. The individual shuttles, spaced on 48-foot centers, extend out over the ship's hatches for loading.

Loading under the shuttles on a thousand-footer is a good place to be if you are a deckhand because you don't have to shift the boat. You may have a shovel full or two of pellets to scrape off the deck, but for most of the 10- to 12-hour load the job is pretty quiet. In a former life, the *American Spirit* (*George A. Stinson*) was owned by National Steel and made regular runs from Duluth-Superior to Zug Island on the Detroit River. Today, the *American Spirit* goes to Zug Island, as well as Nanticoke, Ontario, and Indiana Harbor.

On the lower lakes, taconite brought down from the upper lakes for steel mills at Cleveland and inland locations is stockpiled near the harbor entrance. Ships going up the Cuyahoga River for Arcelor-Mittal's blast furnaces load at the Cleveland Bulk Terminal. The 634-foot *American Republic* was built specifically to make the Cuyahoga shuttle runs from the lakefront to the upper dock. When they're on the shuttle run the *Republic* often operates with two captains because of the short turn-around time.

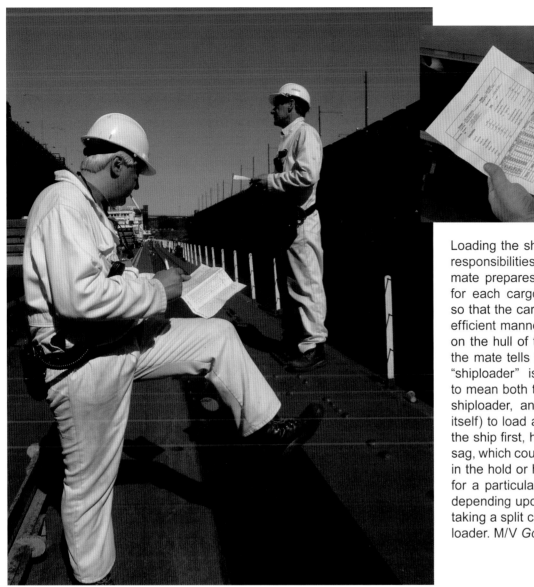

Loading the ship is one of the primary responsibilities of the 1st Mate. The mate prepares the ship's loading plan for each cargo. A load plan is made so that the cargo is loaded in the most efficient manner without placing stress on the hull of the ship. For example, if the mate tells the shiploader (the term "shiploader" is used interchangeably to mean both the person operating the shiploader, and the actual shiploader itself) to load all of the middle holds of the ship first, he may cause the ship to sag, which could create stress fractures in the hold or hull of the ship. The plan for a particular cargo will vary slightly depending upon the dock, if the ship is taking a split cargo, or the type of shiploader. M/V *Gordon C. Leitch*

2nd Mate Bob Slight of Pittsburgh monitors the loading at Cedarville on the *Philip R. Clarke*.

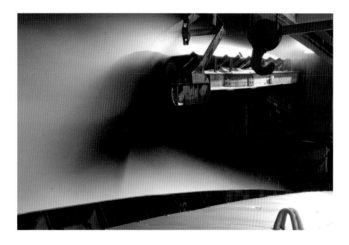

Most of the pellets produced and loaded at Cyprus Northshore's Silver Bay facility are destined for delivery at Cleveland.

Steam created from moist pellets envelops the deck of the *American Victory* during a cool fall evening at Silver Bay. Captains have reported seeing steam still rising from the cargo hold vents down on Lake Erie after loading at Silver Bay.

The delivery of iron ore to steel mills on the lower lakes is not just the domain of the thousand-foot class of vessels. While many large mills are located along the waterfront to take advantage of large bulk shipments by vessel, many mills are located inland, accessible only by smaller ships transiting rivers such as the Rouge or the Cuyahoga. The Great Lakes steamship is still a valuable contributor to this trade. Steamers haul approximately 10 million tons of iron ore yearly for the steel industry. The steamer *Kaye E. Barker* loads pellets at Escanaba, destined for Indiana Harbor. The port of Indiana Harbor, home to ArcelorMittal Steel, receives the largest amount of iron ore shipped on the Great Lakes.

The *Lee A. Tregurtha* has one of the most colorful histories of any ship on the Great Lakes. Under construction as a fuel tanker in 1942 the vessel was requisitioned for service during World War II before it was even launched. As the USS *Chiwawa*, the 501-foot tanker saw extensive duty during the war. Later, in 1961, the vessel was converted for use on the lakes as an ore carrier by the Cleveland-Cliffs Iron Company and renamed the *Walter A. Sterling*.

Marquette, Michigan, to Severstal's Steel mill on the Rouge River, and Escanaba, Michigan, to Indiana Harbor, Indiana, are the main trade routes for the *Lee A. Tregurtha*. The *Tregurtha*, loading at the chute dock at Duluth, has a cargo capacity of nearly 30,000 tons at summer draft.

Over the length of its career the *Lee A. Tregurtha* has steadily gotten longer. During its conversion for use on the lakes the vessel grew just over 228 feet to an overall length of 730 feet. In 1976 the *Tregurtha* was lengthened an additional 96 feet, making it the longest steamship on the Great Lakes, a distinction it held until 2006 when the vessel was converted from a steamer to a diesel-powered ship. This view of the *Tregurtha* shows most of the 24 hatches on the spar deck.

During the loading process the vessel may need to be "shifted" along the dock. Shifting the vessel is done to align the ship's hatch openings with the dock's loading chutes or equipment. For example, loading spouts attached to a grain elevator are only able to reach a certain distance over the deck of the ship. In this instance, for the mate on the *Algocape* to load all of the holds he must move the ship forward or backward along the dock so that the spouts can reach all of the cargo hatches. The mate on duty, working with the deckhands, moves the ship along the dock with the mooring wires payed out or hauled in with the winches. Oftentimes a wire is set so that it slips beneath mooring cleats on the dock without needing the assistance of the deckhands.

On the massive iron ore docks of Lake Superior the chutes were centered every 12 feet. The hatches on Great Lakes ships are centered every 24 feet, thus for a ship to load at an ore dock it has to shift forward or back to accommodate the centering of the ore chutes. Today, many shiploaders move on rails but the design of the loading deck remains the same today as it was a hundred years ago.

The movement of coal for the power industry accounts for about 95 percent of the coal shipped on the Great Lakes. Detroit Edison's Midwest Energy Terminal ships over 20 million tons of low sulfur coal annually from Superior, Wisconsin. Mined in the Powder River and Hanna basins of Wyoming, the bituminous and sub-bituminous coal is used for electrical generation and industrial customers. M/V *Charles M. Beeghly*

Eastern, high bituminous coal is shipped north from Toledo to power plants and industries throughout the Great Lakes Basin. The Toledo facility is owned and operated by CSX Corporation. The movement of coal by rail and through its waterfront terminals accounts for nearly 25 percent of CSX's total revenue. Coal consumption in the United States is currently at about 1.1 billion tons and is expected to increase to about 1.6 billion tons by 2020. S/S *Kaye E. Barker*

Thunder Bay Terminals, a subsidiary of Russel Metals, Inc. ships low sulfur coal mined in Canada's western provinces for thermal power generating customers, as well as metallurgical coal. Just over a million tons of coal is shipped from the facility annually. Metallurgical coal, mined in British Columbia, is generally used to produce hard coke, which is used in the steel-making process. M/V *Algosteel*

Over 35 percent of the coal loaded at U.S. ports goes cross-lake to Canadian customers for the generation of electrical power or the production of steel. Coal is the second largest cargo by tonnage shipped on the Great Lakes. The *Algosoo*, a Canadian self-unloading bulk carrier, loads hydro coal at Midwest Energy.

Coal pours into the hold of the *Algosteel* at Thunder Bay, Ontario. The holds on most lake carriers are sloped so that the cargo will easily flow to the unloading gates. When the gates are opened the coal drops onto the tunnel conveyor belt running beneath the cargo hold.

The *Algorail* usually carries iron ore, limestone, sand, and other aggregate commodities on the lower lakes and St. Lawrence Seaway. The ship occasionally travels north for several loads of coal, although at 640 feet, the *Algorail* is not ideally sized for loading coal on a long-term basis.

On the Great Lakes the shipment of coal follows two main trade patterns. High bituminous, eastern coal generally moves north and west from ports on Lake Erie to the upper Great Lakes, usually as a back-haul cargo after a load of ore or limestone is delivered. Low-sulfur, western coal moves downward from Lake Superior to all of the lower lakes and occasionally to ports on the St. Lawrence Seaway or eastern seaboard. Because of its high cubic volume, the majority of coal loaded for power generation is put onto the larger, 1,000-foot vessels or Seaway self-unloaders. Steamships account for only about 15 percent of the coal moved on the lakes.

Every shiploading facility on the Great Lakes has someone who loads the boat. Whether this is done by gravity chutes, grain spouts, salt funnels or conveyor belts, they work in tandem with the ship's 1st Mate to load the ship in the safest and most efficient manner possible. Rarely, however, does the person running the loading controls stand on the ship's deck. At the Midwest Energy Terminal a portable unit is hand-controlled by the operator directly from the vessel deck. The vessel loading plan is written in chalk on the loading chute so that the shiploader knows the proper loading sequence for the vessel. Loaders work particular ships based on their level of experience. As the shiploading system ages, plans are in the design stages for a replacement loader that may change the current loading scenario. When Midwest Energy first opened, their vessel loader was seated in a small cab high above deck level, but several factors induced the firm to change. High winds were an issue, particularly when climbing up the shiploader in the winter. And the small cab, with barely enough room for one person, lacked facilities that could periodically interrupt loading. So, for safety and worker convenience, the use of the hand-held remote was initiated. M/V *Charles M. Beeghly*

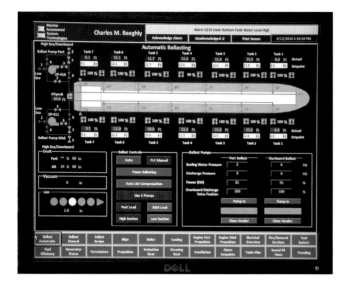

While a ship is empty or light, ballast water is carried to keep the ship from riding too high out of the water. In rough weather this ballast also helps stabilize the ship and keep the ship's propeller in the water. When it comes time to load the ship, the ballast water needs to be removed from the ship's ballast tanks. The main ballast tanks are usually located on the port and starboard sides. Smaller tanks are located forward, aft, or beneath the cargo hold. The *Charles M. Beeghly*, an 806-foot freighter, has 14 main ballast tanks. On the *Beeghly* the ballast controls are fully automated, a feature that was added during a 2009 engine room overhaul.

High calcium limestone pours into the hold of the *Joseph L Block* at Port Inland, Michigan. Limestone is made primarily of two minerals: calcite (calcium carbonite) and dolomite (calcium and magnesium carbonate). The amount of magnesium carbonate determines how the limestone is classified. High calcium limestone, used as a fluxing agent in the steel-making process, contains less than 5 percent magnesium carbonate.

The *Joseph L. Block* is on its 39th trip of the season. This load of limestone is destined for the CN ore dock at Duluth. From Duluth the limestone is shipped by rail to a taconite processing plant on the iron range. The mixture of high calcium limestone and dolomite limestone are blended with the taconite to produce a flux pellet for use in blast furnaces.

The Port Inland limestone quarry is owned and operated by the Belgian-based firm Carmeuse Natural Chemicals. Carmeuse operates a high calcium quarry as well as a crushing and processing plant at Port Inland, producing over 6 million tons of aggregate annually. The *Block* will take half of a split load of 13,450 GT of high cal limestone here from a single, fixed position shiploader before proceeding to Carmeuse's Cedarville dock to complete the load with 13,450 GT of dolomite.

The ATB *Dorothy Ann* and barge *Pathfinder* load 6AA washed limestone at Port Calcite at Rogers City, Michigan. The *Pathfinder* is the cargo section and forward end of the former steamer *J. L. Mauthe*. The *Mauthe* was launched in 1952 and was one of the last straight-decked vessels left in the American lakes fleet before its conversion to a tug-barge. The *Pathfinder* carries over 2 million tons of cargo annually.

The loading rig at Calcite can load between 2,500 to 3,000 tons per hour into the hold of a ship. The loading belt extends across the width of the deck to fill the hold, but the rig itself is stationary so the vessel must shift up and down the dock during the loading process. It will take the *Pathfinder* about ten hours to complete this load of 20,000 tons for a customer in Marine City.

The quarry at Rogers City is the largest open pit limestone quarry in the world. Production at the Calcite quarry began in 1912 for the Michigan Limestone and Chemical Company. In 2008 the quarry and processing plant became part of Carmeuse's North American operations. The early history of the Great Lakes self-unloader can be traced back to Michigan Limestone. Beginning in 1912, the firm built three self-unloaders for the stone trade. Here, the mate on the *Pathfinder* keeps in contact with the vessel loader as the rig banks the cargo into the corner of the hatch opening.

Over the past five years Great Lakes ships have carried over 36 million tons of stone products, the majority of it from American ports. Located just outside of Cedarville, Michigan, is Carmeuse's Port Dolomite limestone quarry. Port Dolomite is a major shipping port for limestone in Michigan's Upper Peninsula. Loading here on its 26th trip of the season, the *Philip R. Clarke* takes on a 25,000 net ton cargo of dolomite destined for Duluth.

Dolomite pouring into the cargo hold of the *Philip R. Clarke* at Cedarville. The shore side shiploading rig itself moves along the dock on a set of rails while the shuttle can extend over the deck of the ship across the width of the hatch opening.

In addition to smaller crushed stone, massive limestone boulders weighing up to 30 tons are also shipped from Port Dolomite.

The *Arthur M. Anderson* takes on a load of Rotary B kiln stone at LaFarge's Stoneport loading facility on Lake Huron. The Presque Isle Quarry was acquired by the Lafarge Corporation in July of 2000. Over 7 million tons of stone are shipped from the quarry annually. Lafarge also operates aggregate facilities at Meldrum Bay, Ontario, and at Marblehead, Ohio. About 50 percent of the limestone quarried at Presque Isle is delivered for metallurgical use with the other half being used in the aggregate industry.

Crushed limestone for use in rotary kilns ranges in size from 1/4-inch to 2 1/2 inches. In the kiln the limestone is heated to temperatures up to 1,300 degrees Fahrenheit to produce lime.

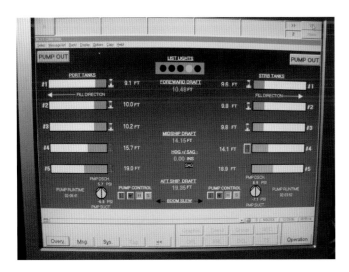

The ballast water that is carried when the ship is light is pumped out of the tanks during loading. A computer screen displays the ballast status on the Canadian bulker *John D. Leitch*, showing the levels in the tanks, as well as the vessel draft forward, midship, and aft.

The water depth in the ballast tanks is marked on a soundings board. Sounding boards are usually found in the ship's pilothouse and on the deck so that the mate can easily see it.

Ballast water being pumped out the starboard side of the *John D. Leitch* at Duluth.

There is no room for complacency on a ship, and although modern technology can show the water level in the ship's ballast tanks on a computer display screen, sounding tanks is a regular part of the loading process. Ballast tanks contain a sounding pipe that is open at the bottom. A steel rod, marked with a chalk-like paste, is lowered into the pipe. When the water hits the paste it changes its color and indicates the water depth in the tank.

Load lights are general indicators of whether the ship is trim. The lights are mounted forward and aft on the ship in an easy-to-see location.

During the loading process the final draft of the vessel is the critical factor in determining how much cargo is loaded. Ships loading on Lake Superior for ports on the lower lakes are restricted by the water draft of the St. Marys River. The water draft for lakers at mid-summer is usually around 25.5 feet. The draft is also regulated by the port or dock where the cargo is going to be discharged, or by a river that may need to be navigated to reach a dock. It is rare that a Great Lakes ship is loaded to its maximum tonnage capacity. When the loading nears completion the mate keeps a close eye on the overall draft of the ship. Draft numbers are painted on the hull forward, midship and aft. All numbers are a uniform 6 inches tall and are spaced 6 inches apart. Here, the mate on the *American Republic* checks the ship's draft as it loads at Cleveland's lakefront dock for a shuttle up the Cuyahoga.

The Port of Thunder Bay is one of Canada's largest export centers for grain produced on the Canadian prairies. Grain arrives by rail to the port where it is stored in mammoth terminal elevators for delivery to eastern markets or overseas destinations. Domestic shipments are loaded into "flatbacks," the Canadian equivalent of the American straight-decker. These Seaway-sized ships are 730 to 735 feet in length, 72 to 75 feet in beam and carry between 25 to 30,000 metric tons of grain. M/V *Algocape*

Prior to the opening of the St. Lawrence Seaway System the movement of grain within the Great Lakes ranked as the largest commodity next to iron ore. Even before the discovery of iron-bearing land, grain was the cargo that defined export shipping on the lakes. Wheat was the first of the major grains grown in the Upper Midwest and became the staple product delivered from the prairies to burgeoning ports like Toledo, Chicago, and Milwaukee, followed later by Duluth, Superior, and the Canadian port towns of Fort William and Port Arthur. Grain flowed eastward to Buffalo, New York, for milling to feed the ravenous markets along the eastern seaboard.

The movement of Canadian grain through the Great Lakes is about 30 percent of the total Canadian annual output. The principal market destinations for Canadian grain are Western Europe, North Africa, the Middle East, and Latin America. Grain loaded Canadian lakers are unloaded along the Seaway at Montreal, Quebec City, Baie Comeau and Port Cartier. M/V *Canadian Miner*

Rail transportation is the ship's biggest competitor in the eastward movement of grain. In recent years rail shipments to millers in Ontario and Quebec have cut into the Canadian laker market because of their ability to deliver smaller quantities on a steady basis so that the miller does not need large storage facilities. Year-round delivery is also not impacted by the seasonal closing of the St. Lawrence Seaway. M/V *Canadian Miner*

The opening of the St. Lawrence Seaway System in 1959, the continued evolution of rail service and the unit train, and the growth of deep sea ports along the Gulf coast have all contributed to the rapid decline of the American Great Lakes grain trade. Changes in rail concessions and the development of Vancouver, British Columbia, as a deep water port have had a similar affect on the Canadian Great Lakes trade, although not to the same degree. M/V *Canadian Miner*

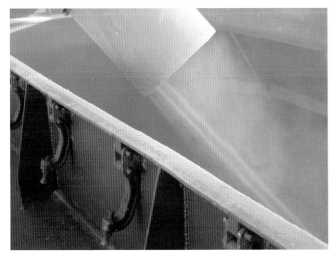

Grain is loaded at Thunder Bay from nine terminal elevators into lakers and ocean-going vessels. Only about 10 percent of the 1.2 million tons loaded onto ships at Thunder Bay goes into lakers; the remaining grain is loaded aboard salt water vessels for direct overseas shipment. The increase of direct rail shipments to eastern Canada, combined with shipments via ocean-going vessels, has resulted in the scrapping of a number of Canadian bulk carriers in the past decade. S/S *Montrealais*

Wheat, barley, rye, and corn, along with oil seeds such as canola, flaxseed, and mustard seed are among the many grains loaded onto Canadian lakers throughout the shipping season. Grain is loaded into ships at rates of 3,000 to 4,000 tons per hour. American lake vessels account for only a very small part of grain shipments on the lakes. Typical cargoes shipped from American ports include wheat, barley, corn, and soybeans. In the late 1990s self-unloaders entered into the grain trade, loading cargoes for Buffalo, with an occasional transit of the St. Lawrence Seaway. M/V *Maritime Trader*

Taking care of the ship is an age old job of the mariner that surpasses all time and history. The ship is home and some while some captains and crew have differences of opinion in how that ideal translates to labor, most sailors take pride in their vessel and work to keep it clean and well cared for. M/V *Canadian Transport*

Most painting is done while the ship is on the run between ports. On twenty-four 24-hour runs across Lake Superior or Michigan the crew usually gets some painting time. Crew members on ships with short runs and turnaround usually have less time to paint, or sleep. S/S *Kaye E. Barker*

Ships are painted certain colors for a reason...they get dirty. Ore ships are usually red, colliers are black, while stone and cement haulers usually have gray decks. Touch-ups and painting continue throughout the regular season. M/V *Indiana Harbor*

Extracted from deep below the surface of the earth, salt mined at Goderich, Ontario, pours into the holds of ships as if being sifted from a giant shaker. Salt accounts for about 20 percent of the annual tonnage on the Great Lakes, at just under 6 million tons. Salt is used for highway deicing (rock salt), brine, and table salt, as well as other industrial uses. M/V *Algomarine*

Salt is mined at Goderich 1,800 feet below the surface, roughly the height of the famous Toronto space needle. The salt rock is loosened with dynamite, then crushed and screened before being brought to the surface. A cubic yard of salt weighs about one ton, so moving salt by water is the most economical means. One shipload of salt is equivalent to using 60 trucks. M/V *Algomarine*

A fine layer of white looks deceptively like frost, but the air temperature hovers near 32 degrees Celsius (89° Fahrenheit). The *Algomarine* makes regular runs into Goderich to load salt. On this trip the cargo is a split load of treated C, untreated C, and AA salt destined for customers in Milwaukee and Chicago. Salt is delivered from above ground storage sheds via conveyor line to the shiploader, a large vertical chute, for loading onto the vessel.

Ship's stores come in all shapes and sizes. Barrels of lube oil are lowered from the poop deck of the *Canadian Miner* down to the engine room gangway while the ship loads at Superior. M/V *Canadian Miner*

A home-made track and cart are used on the *American Integrity* to ferry engine room supplies from the dock to the ship. M/V *American Integrity*

Galley supplies are taken aboard at the dock when possible. Because this impacts their bottom line (being fed), crew members are always eager to help unload the pallets. M/V *Indiana Harbor*

As the holds are filled the hatch covers are methodically placed back on top of the hatch coamings in preparation for departure. The ship's bosun is responsible for making sure the deck hands are kept busy handling lines, securing hatch covers, clearing away any material that may have fallen onto the deck, and stowing any equipment or supplies used while the ship was loading. When it comes time to leave no one wants to keep the captain waiting.

Using the engine controls on the starboard bridge wing, the captain of the *Indiana Harbor* keeps an eye on the dock at Superior's Midwest Energy Terminal while the ship's mooring lines are released. To keep the ship up against the dock the captain uses his bow and stern thrusters in combination with the main engine until the crew are safely aboard the ship. Once the ship is away from the dock the captain switches the engine controls from the bridge wing to the main pilothouse console.

Each ship has over a thousand hatch clamps that need to be closed for every voyage. It's with good reason that deck hands refer to the spar deck of the ship as the hatch farm. In inclement weather the clamps are always secured before the ship departs the dock. On a calm summer day they are sometimes done on the run as the ship is departing. With three to four deck hands it doesn't take too long to secure the deck for the voyage.

Once the ship is loaded the journey begins to the unloading port. Within the Great Lakes it is no more than a three-day trip. For ships traveling the St. Lawrence Seaway it could be seven to ten days. The *Canadian Transport* departs DTE's Midwest Energy Terminal at Superior with low sulfur coal destined for Ontario Power Generation's Nanticoke plant on Lake Erie, about a two-and-a-half-day run.

The movement of iron ore continues to be the focal point of American shipping on the Great Lakes. After departing the Severstal Dearborn dock on the Rouge River the *Kaye E. Barker* makes its way through the Dix Avenue bascule bridge. S/S *Kaye E. Barker*

The stone trade takes vessels across all five of the Great Lakes and is the closest approximation these ships come to being truly employed as tramp steamers. The *Manistee* departs its berth at Duluth's Hallett 8 dock for a one-hour shift over to the CN ore dock to load taconite. M/V *Manistee*

CHAPTER 4:
Ships at Work: Trip Cycle— Underway

From the head of the St. Lawrence River at Wolff Island, to Point Iroquois and the turn into Whitefish Bay, the five Great Lakes are strung together like jewels by a series of rivers and canals. The connecting waterways of the Great Lakes are the strands of water through which float the commerce of two nations, as well as ships from around the world. The Welland Canal connects Lake Ontario with Lake Erie, bypassing the mighty Niagara Falls.

Once the ship is loaded the captain takes the vessel out of the harbor and heads to the unloading destination. This portion of the cycle may take three to five hours, or three to five days.

From fit-out in March until lay-up in mid-January, traffic managers have vessels in motion all over the lakes. On any given day they could have a ship at an ore dock on Lake Superior, or underway up-bound from Lake Michigan after delivering a load, with another winding its way up the Rouge River to unload at the same time that one is loading coal at Sandusky for delivery on Lake Michigan before heading to Escanaba for more ore.

If all goes smoothly everything will change or move in a different direction in six to twelve hours. That's a big 'if,' however. Delays from weather occur; perhaps the St. Mary's River is closed because of fog. There may already be another ship at the dock, meaning a ten-hour wait for a berth. Maybe one of the ships has engine trouble and needs to go into a shipyard for repair. In the spring the ship could be caught in ice, or the taconite pellets are frozen and need to be thawed before they can be loaded. There are always multiple possibilities.

Ships down-bound from Lake Superior are usually going to be making a longer trip. The cargoes will be iron ore pellets (taconite), low-sulfur coal, or grain. It takes about 24 hours for a ship to cross Lake Superior from Duluth-Superior to the Soo; slightly less for a vessel departing Thunder Bay. For a ship going to the Soo Locks from Marquette with iron ore, it's about a 12-hour run.

Once clear of the Soo Locks it is about a 6-hour passage down the St. Mary's River to Lake Huron. At DeTour lighthouse the down-bound vessel may head west toward the Straits of Mackinac before turning south for the 24-hour run to the steel mills along at South Chicago and Indiana. A ship loaded with grain will likely head south from DeTour, taking the 16-hour ride across Lake Huron before entering the Rivers en-route to Lake Erie.

The down-bound vessels deliver most of their cargoes of taconite to docks at Cleveland and Conneaut on the American side, and Nanticoke, Ontario, on the Canadian border. Eastern coal heads north as a backhaul out of Lake Erie from Toledo, Sandusky, Conneaut and Ashtabula for distribution to power generation plants and private industries throughout the Great Lakes basin.

Lakes Huron and Michigan are the focal points of the Great Lakes stone and cement trade. Ships moving aggregates stay close in to shore, hopping in and out of Stone-port, Rogers City, Cedarville, Port Inland, Meldrum Bay and Alpena to shuttle cargoes down to docks on the St. Clair River, to Detroit and Windsor, or up and around the Straits to Manistee, Muskegon, Holland, St. Joseph, South Chicago, Milwaukee and Green Bay.

Ships heading down the St. Lawrence Seaway head east at the Detroit River Light, crossing Lake Erie before entering the Welland Canal at Port Colborne. Then, 8 to 10 hours later they enter Lake Ontario, taking the mid-lake route past the gleaming Toronto skyline to the north and the wooded New York countryside to the south. Most domestic grain boats coming off the lakes head north toward Quebec City, Baie Comeau, or Port Cartier before returning inland. At any given time on the Great Lakes during the shipping season there is always a ship on the move somewhere.

Collectively known as "the rivers," the long narrow stretch of water connecting Lake Erie to Lake Huron includes the Detroit River, Lake St. Clair and the St. Clair River. The venerable steamer *Kaye E. Barker* enters the head of the St. Clair River at Port Huron, running the route that could easily be called the iron ore highway. It was through this connecting waterway that the ore needed to fuel our nation during World War II moved non-stop from the upper lakes to the blast furnaces on the lower lakes.

Green sailors are still sent up to the lock master to get the "keys to the locks" on their first trip through the Soo. The locks at Sault Ste. Marie are an engineering marvel, completing the Seaway's final 21- foot climb from sea level the to the level of Lake Superior. Two locks transfer the entire up and down-bound tonnage, but the Poe Lock, the larger of the two American locks, handles almost 75 percent of the traffic. A new lock is in the preliminary stages of development, the first major expansion in three decades.

The *Wilfred Sykes* makes its way out of the Calumet River in South Chicago. The Calumet is a prime example of a waterway that has been changed and re-shaped to accommodate the needs of heavy industry. The elevators and steels mills have closed as the face of industry has changed, giving way to smaller operations—coal docks, scrap yards, bulk storage areas, and empty fields sandwiched between bascule bridges.

The deep blue waters of the Great Lakes create a tantalizing desire to jump in. Spectacular vistas are one of the enjoyable parts of sailing on the lakes. It takes anywhere from 24 to 30 hours for a ship to cross Lake Superior, 24 to run the north-south length of Lake Michigan, and 16 hours for the down-bound run from DeTour to Port Huron across Lake Huron. Vast stretches of pure, fresh water are a hallmark of the Great Lakes. M/V *American Republic*

Slow getting in the locks, fast moving in between... transiting the Welland is a ritual repeated all season by Canadian ships. Ships maximized for the locks on the St. Lawrence Seaway, like the Canadian bulk carrier *CSL Laurentien* entering Lock 7 on the Welland Canal, go full ahead into the lock; the water they're displacing has little room to slip behind to make room.

If you travel by ship then the likelihood of things coming to you by ship, like mail, goes up. The Great Lakes has the only ship with its own zip code. The *J. W. Westcott II* delivers mail and serves as a water taxi for crews on the Detroit River. At Sault Ste. Marie, just below the Soo Locks on the St. Marys River, the supply ship *Ojibway* tenders food, lube oil, engine parts, and parcels to ships. All of these transfers are done on the run, day or night, throughout the shipping season.

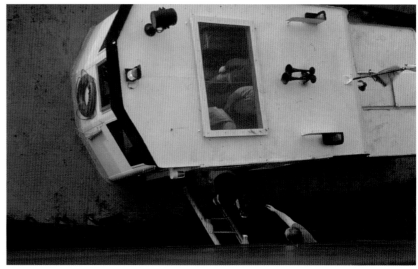

Safety at sea is everyone's responsibility and training is mandatory both on and off the ship. A fire aboard the ship is very serious business. Each crew member is assigned a fire station and a duty to perform in the event of a fire. Fire fighting plans are contained in an easily accessible area outside of the ship's cabins, along with hoses, axes, and CO_2 and dry chemical extinguishers. Most crew members are also sent to fire fighting school during the off-season.

The accumulation of dangerous gases can also occur from certain cargoes or during a fire. On-board training in the use of self-contained breathing apparatus is conducted on a regular basis. On the deck of the *Indiana Harbor* the ship's 1st Mate goes over the basics of using SCBA equipment with two maritime students from the SIU (Seafarer's International Union) school at Piney Point, Maryland. M/V *Indiana Harbor*

A Seaway self-unloader up-bound on Whitefish Bay.

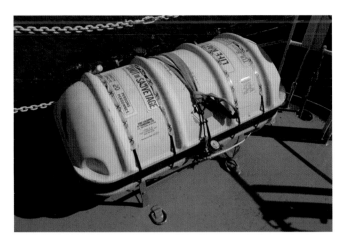 

All mariners live with the knowledge that one day they may have to abandon ship. In the event that such a catastrophe may occur, ships are equipped with every possible means of saving lives. Vessels on the lakes carry a combination of boats for this purpose. Older ships carry two open life boats located on both the port and starboard side of the after end. Newer ships have an enclosed lifeboat secured on either the port or starboard side of the ship next to the berthing accommodations. Rafts that hold 10 to 25 people are secured in hydrostatically released canisters on the ship's deck. These life rafts are equipped with emergency equipment and supplies in compliance with the international SOLAS convention (Safety of Life at Sea). Immersion suits are provided to each member of the crew. The suits are designed to provide thermal protection in the water and wick excess moisture away from the body. A mariner entering 32-degree Fahrenheit water has an estimated 6-hour survival window wearing an immersion suit. In addition, life rings are stationed along deck housings and railings on the ship's exterior in the event of someone falling overboard.

H2O hydrostatic release on life canister opens at 5 to 15 feet.

A view looking down on a lifeboat. Lifeboats are equipped with oars, rope, lights, flares, first aid supplies, several days' worth of food and water and other emergency equipment. Successfully lowering a lifeboat into the water can be difficult depending upon sea conditions. Crew members in an open lifeboat are also totally exposed to the weather. M/V *Voyageur Pioneer*

Maritime literature is riddled with stories of the open boat. Some entail astonishing feats of navigation, the most famous of those belonging to William Bligh and 18 of his men set adrift from the *HMS Bounty* for seven weeks and 3,700 miles. The Great Lakes are a far distance from the temperate waters of the South Pacific and survival here in an open boat is critically reduced by the temperature of both the air and the waters of the lakes. The familiarity of releasing the lifeboat from the davits and knowing how to properly use lifesaving equipment can be the difference between life and death. Fire and lifeboat drills are mandatory on Great Lakes ships.

Swinging a lifeboat out during a drill. M/V *Maritime Trader*

An emergency rescue launch being lowered. S/S *Philip R. Clarke*

The crew of the *Cason J. Callaway* takes a turn at the oars. Steering a lifeboat is done with the use of an oar referred to as a sweep oar.

CHAPTER 4:
Ships at Work: Trip Cycle— Unloading

Not more than a generation ago a ship would be in port for a day or two unloading its cargo. Massive dock side machinery would be involved in removing the cargo from the holds of the ships. When the buckets and clamshells could reach no further, dozens of men were employed between the cavernous walls of steel to shovel and clear the hold of every last piece of cargo. M/V *H. Lee White*

The proliferation of self-unloading systems has changed the face of shipping on the Great Lakes in a number of ways. First and foremost, nearly every ship on both the American and Canadian side of the lakes has this technology. The days of the "classic" laker with the pilot house forward, cabins and stack back aft, with a long, lean open deck between, are almost a thing of the past. Secondly, self-unloading technology has eliminated the need for shore side equipment to remove the cargo, reducing unloading time from days in some cases, to a matter of hours in most. The gantry cranes and Hulett unloaders are now relegated to the scrap heap or memorialized as museum pieces. This rapid unloading time also has a direct impact on the ship's crew by reducing the amount of time in port. This change makes it more difficult for many to go "up the street," virtually eliminating the transient sailor of past generations and making it harder to spend time at home with family, or perform maintenance and upkeep on the ship.

The unloading process begins almost immediately when the ship arrives at the dock. Hatch covers are being removed as mooring lines are being secured. The ship's boom is swung over the dock while the conveyorman powers up the unloading system. In the tunnel the gateman is starting the pneumatic vibrators on the walls of the holds to help keep the cargo flowing once the gates are opened.

Unless some assistance from the dock is needed to spot the location for the discharge pile, there are few people on the dock, especially if it's the middle of the morning. In some respects it's almost a covert operation when a ship arrives at night and is gone long before the sun is up and the plant workers arrive in the morning.

On the ship the mates and wheelsmen will work their standard watch. The deckhands will work during the unload rinsing the holds, taking soundings, replacing hatch covers, or shifting the lines if needed. Some of the crew may get to go home for a few hours if they can get someone to take their watch for them.

Unloading the cargo is the main duty for the ship's conveyorman and the gateman. They will work through the entire unload until the cargo is off the ship. If it is a long unload, the GPMRs, or equivalent, will assist in the cargo tunnel opening gates.

Working the ship's unloading tunnel is the modern day equivalent of being a coal passer. It is a tough job. The unloading tunnel is located at the bottom of the ship. In the fall and winter there's frost on the outside walls; in the spring, moist pellets create layers of fog that run the length of the tunnel; in the summer the heat can bring a bead of sweat in an instant. Cleaning up after the cargo is off the boat adds rivers of red or black water to an already grimy underworld. Taconite-stained clothing is the style of the day for the gateman and unloading crew.

If everything goes well it takes about 6 to 10 hours to offload an average cargo of coal, taconite, or stone. At the end of the unload the boom is secured to the deck, the belts shut down and the crew get some rest if they can before the next port, as the next trip of the season begins.

The stone trade brought the evolution of the self-unloading vessel to the forefront of the Great Lakes transportation industry. Sinuous booms of rectangular metal held fast to the ship with thick strands of wire reached out over the dock, stone falling from the end into a conical pile eventually reaching to the height of the ship's pilothouse. By the 1990s, few (if any) remnants of the old shore side equipment remain. What used to take days is finished in a matter of hours. S/S *John G. Munson*

There is little time wasted in the unloading process. As soon as the ship arrives at the dock and the lines are secure, the conveyorman is firing up the generators that will power the unloading system. If any of the crew is lucky enough to be going home they get off the ship as quickly as they can. Once the cargo starts to fall from the hold onto the belts the unloading systems can continuously deliver several thousand tons an hour. Twenty thousand tons of salt can be put on the dock in about six hours. M/V *Canadian Transport*

The main components of a self-unloading system are a sloped cargo hold, a belt conveyor system beneath the hold in the cargo tunnel, an incline or a loop belt to pull the cargo up from the tunnel, and an unloading boom and conveyor belt to discharge the cargo onto the dock. The average length of an unloading boom is 250 feet. Some ships have longer booms but none exceed 300 feet in length. M/V *Indiana Harbor*

One of the advantages of using an unloading boom, besides its long reach, is the ability to pivot it up to 90 degrees to the port or starboard side of the ship. This allows cargo to be dropped at a specific location on the dock with minimal shifting of the vessel. Looking up at the boom on the *Indiana Harbor* shows the near 90-degree extension over the port side of the vessel.

Open dock spaces on the lower lakes, such as the Pinney Dock at Ashtabula, Ohio, are used for discharging the ships cargo of taconite. At multi-modal facilities like this the ore is then loaded onto rail cars for delivery to steel mills farther inland, completing the supply chain cycle. Commodities are stockpiled late in the season for delivery during the winter months when the shipping season shuts down. M/V *Indiana Harbor*

The A-frame shape of a modern unloading boom is a combination of tubular steel and aluminum. The boom is raised or lowered with a hydraulic cylinder attached to a vertical pin stepped onto the deck at either the forward or after end of the ship. The hydraulic cylinder is approximately 21 inches in diameter and weighs around 22 tons. A lifted boom with a full load of cargo running on the belt can weigh up to 200 tons. S/S *American Valor*

The conveyorman monitors the ship's unloading system during unloading and is responsible for maintaining the system and making sure that it operates smoothly during the shipping season. S/S *Kaye E. Barker*

The *Roger Blough* became the first Great Lakes vessel to use a shuttle conveyor unloading system. The shuttle boom, located at the aft end of the ship, receives its cargo from an incline belt fed from the cargo gates. A similar system was installed on the *Stewart J. Cort.* Later, both USS Great Lakes Fleet 1,000-footers, the *Edwin H. Gott* and the *Edgar B. Speer,* were equipped with shuttle boom unloading systems. Shuttle booms are designed to feed taconite into shore side hoppers that in turn feed conveyors that move the pellets into a storage yard. The shuttle system was not widely adapted because of the necessity of having a shore side hopper for receiving the cargo. M/V *Roger Blough*

The end of the shuttle boom where the belt wraps back underneath.

The *Roger Blough*, up-bound in the St. Clair River, is one of the fastest ships on the lakes.

Salt flows from the cargo hold of the steamer *Manistee*. Many ships have a two-belt conveyor system beneath the cargo hold. On the *Manistee* the belts bring the cargo forward where it drops onto a transfer belt which then deposits it into vertically traveling buckets. The bucket elevator lifts the cargo up to a point where the bucket tips it onto the belt (on deck boom) which runs the cargo out onto the dock. S/S *Manistee*

Unloading boom extended over dock.

The *Manistee's* unique chain-driven slewing table used to pivot the unloading boom.

Port incline belt on the *Manistee*.

Sand, gravel, dirt, gypsum, and limestone make up the majority of the over 30 million tons of aggregates shipped yearly on the lakes. Because of the predominance of quarries in Michigan, that state leads the Great Lakes in the shipment of these products. The proximity to water of large quarries at Rogers City, Port Inland, Presque Isle, Cedarville, and Brevort make the movement of stone and sand by ship extremely efficient and cost effective. S/S *John G. Munson*

Roughly 4 inches by 6 inches in size, sugar stone is one of the many size variations of limestone produced from Michigan quarries. The shipment of limestone accounts for over 80 percent of all aggregates moved on the Great Lakes. Most aggregate products are unloaded onto open dock spaces for transshipment by rail or truck for use in the agricultural, construction, and cement industries. S/S *John G. Munson*

Limestone is considered a back-haul cargo for ships traveling north to Lake Superior. The *John G. Munson*, unloading limestone here at Hallett Dock 8 in Superior, will depart for Two Harbors to load iron ore when the discharge is complete. The *Munson* loaded this 24,000-ton cargo at Port Calcite in Rogers City. S/S *John G. Munson*

A self-unloading vessel the size of the *John G. Munson* can discharge its 24,000 tons of cargo in about 6 hours. Hydraulically operated gates at the bottom of the cargo hold, when opened, allow the cargo to slide down the sloped walls of the hold and onto the unloading belt(s) running beneath.

The ship's cargo tunnel is located beneath the cargo holds. This view of the starboard side tunnel on the *Munson* shows the sloped inboard side of the hold with the conveyor belt running beneath.

Sugar stone climbs out of the darkened tunnel up an incline belt where it falls onto a transfer belt that will deposit the stone to the bucket elevator. The *Munson's* unloading system discharges the cargo at a rate of 4- to 6-thousand tons per hour.

At the end of the incline belt the sugar stone tumbles into a hopper that drops it onto a transfer belt which feeds the bucket elevator.

From the short transfer belt the sugar stone is lifted out of the cargo tunnel by a continuous loop of steel buckets before being deposited on the unloading boom's belt.

The *John G. Munson*, a former Bradley fleet stone carrier, is equipped with a 250-foot forward-mounted unloading boom. Most unloading booms have a maximum radius of 90 degrees—the boom on the *Munson* can move 110 degrees to port or starboard.

Following the flow of the sugar stone from the cargo hold, in the final step the stone is dropped onto the boom's conveyor belt which runs the cargo off the ship to the stockpile on the dock.

The *Munson's* boom is raised and lowered with steel cables. The cables extend from the top of the boom housing to two sheave blocks connected to the steel frame of the unloading boom.

Unloading a bulk carrier requires shore side equipment. For grain cargoes the use of the marine leg has changed little over the past one hundred years. The technology is similar to the bucket elevator idea used on self-unloading ships...a series of small buckets, now plastic instead of tin, lift the grain up the marine belt... elevating it to the top of the elevator.

A marine leg takes a bite out of the grain as it digs into the cargo hold of the *Maritime Trader* at Quebec City.

The *Herbert C. Jackson* unloads into the hopper at Marquette. The *Jackson* usually will load iron ore at Marquette for the Rouge and then return with eastern coal as a backhaul from Toledo or Sandusky to ports like Muskegon or Marquette.

There are nearly 5,500 cubic miles of water in the Great Lakes, yet low water levels in recent years have greatly reduced the efficiency of both the American and Canadian fleets. The impact of low water levels has been exacerbated by the lack of an adequate dredging program for ports and harbors on the Great Lakes; a condition resulting in vessels loading well short of their carrying capacity. Depending upon the size of the ship, every inch of cargo left behind results in a loss of tonnage. For a thousand-footer, one inch of cargo is equal to 207 tons. For a Seaway-sized vessel that same inch of cargo is equal to 115 tons.

In spite of low water levels, the movement of bulk commodities by ship remains the greenest form of transportation available. For example, 18,000 tons of cargo moved by ship equate to the use of 7,167 gallons of fuel and 1 ton of emissions. The same cargo moved by rail would require 180 cars, 36,350 gallons of fuel and produce 11 tons of emissions, and if by road it would take 692 trucks burning 110,700 gallons of fuel and emitting 16 tons of pollutants, according to facts provided by Wisconsin Commercial Ports Assn.

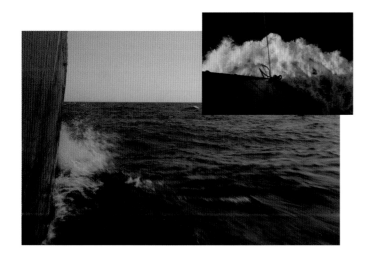

In 2009 the St. Lawrence Seaway celebrated its 50th Anniversary, a milestone for a system that has had its share of success as well as its disappointments. The movement of iron ore, bulk commodities and grain account for the majority of domestic and overseas shipments. Upwards of 200-million metric tonnes of cargo move through the system annually, including nearly 40 percent of Canada's domestic trade. The average shipping season begins in late March, depending upon ice conditions, and closes at the end of December, with 3,000 to 5,000 vessels transiting the system during the season.

An engineer watches from the gangway door as the *Frontenac* works its way through late season ice.

CHAPTER 5:
Hotel and Food Services

Living aboard a ship for six to nine months out of the year is perhaps the most challenging aspect of the job. No matter how you look at it there is no getting around the fact that being away from home means missing social and family events; weddings, births, school conferences, football games, birthdays, anniversaries. It is a part of the job that sailors learn to live with. The job has been likened to being institutionalized, except that you're there of your own accord.

Most crew members have private living quarters on a ship. The captain and chief have a stateroom, plus an office for conducting ship's business. All licensed officers, deck, engineering and the steward, have a stateroom. Unlicensed crew, especially an OS (ordinary seaman), or a wiper or entry-level engine room equivalent, may share rooms. This is determined by the amount of living space available on the ship. Spare berthing quarters are often reserved for service technicians when they need to ride the ship. In the case of deckhands it is usually two per room, which is considerably better than the four to six that used to share quarters decades ago. Most of the rooms are the size of a modest motel room. On some older vessels the shower and toilet facilities are centrally located for the deck department, but the occurrence of that is infrequent.

Food has always been one of the equalizers in the world of the Great Lakes sailor. One of the things that the shipping companies on the Great Lakes have always been conscientious of is feeding the crews that work on the ships. Being away from home for long period of time is difficult but most crews can always look forward to three square meals a day.

Great Lakes ships have the reputation of providing good food. All of the ship's galleys are operated like a shore side restaurant, providing a variety of choices for breakfast, lunch and dinner. The Steward heads the galley staff, which traditionally includes a 2nd Cook, and a porter or steward's assistant.

Like all areas of the ship, the galley has also undergone cost-saving changes in recent years which include cuts in personnel. The ship's porter is the bottom of the hierarchy in the galley, but many vessel owners and operators have begun to do away with porters, placing those responsibilities onto the role of the 2nd Cook. There are a number of Canadian ships that operate with a single person in the galley, literally the "Chief cook and bottle washer." The porter's position was often used as a stepping stone to a 2nd Cook's job and later possibly, a Steward's post, but it is more difficult now to climb that succession ladder on a ship.

Just as it is on shore, some cooks are better than others. You are much more likely to hear if someone is a good cook when you first get on board than you are about the qualifications of a captain or chief engineer. If the crew says you won't starve on this ship, that's a good indication; if the cook's nickname is "meat burner" you have a pretty good idea of what to expect. For the most part, they are all rather good and the food is plentiful. As with the times, healthy choices and low-fat selections are available for those conscientious of their diets while large portions for growing young deckhands are also served to choice.

Social activities on board have changed in the past few decades. Cards, cribbage games, television, and shop activities used to be more popular, but with the growth in personal consumer electronics that has changed. Personal stereos like iPods and CD players are favorites, and many crew now have laptops with cell-phone adaptive Internet links to keep them in touch with everyday life away from the ship, in addition to the cell phone. Many ships also provide satellite television in every room (not a free perk for all, however) so even the group activity of watching VHS movies in the crew lounge have gone away.

With all of the lifestyle changes, the galley remains as the one place where all of the crew can gather outside of the job or their individual rooms. The galley remains the social center of the ship, the central location where all social strata of the ship can exchange conversation, and the ship's steward is often the person on the ship who knows the most because of the constant ebb and flow of chatter among crew mates.

Sailors are justly proud of the ships they sail upon. Many are very accurate historians of their vessels and its particulars. For over a century ships like the one here were built in the Canadian's town of Collingwood, Ontario. The yard was closed in 1986 but many Collingwood-built ships continue to sail the lakes. M/V *Algolake*

Many believe that the ship's bell is the heart and soul of the ship. In this case, the bell from the steamer *Richard M. Marshall* currently resides aboard the steamer *Kaye E. Barker*. The Marshall underwent four name changes before being scrapped, but its bell sails on. S/S *Kaye E. Barker*

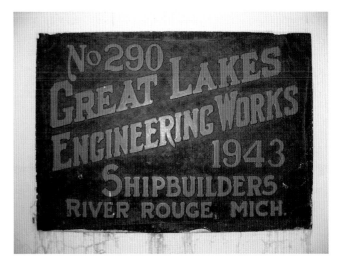

The builder's plaque from the 1943-era vessel *Richard J. Reiss*. One owner of the vessel, built at the Great Lakes Engineering Works on the mouth of the Rouge River in Detroit, removed the middle initial from the name out of a superstition surrounding 13 letters in the name. Today, the vessel sails for Grand River Navigation as the *Manistee*.

The view forward from a room on the *American Integrity*.

Most crew members have their own rooms, especially on the older vessels that were built when crews numbered 28 to 32 men. Reduced crewing has opened up a lot of berthing space. Unlicensed crew members, such as a deckhand with little seniority, are more likely to share rooms.

The ship is the sailor's home away from home and some like to decorate more than others. On ships with the deck cabins set back aft, the crew accommodation decks are usually located between the pilothouse level and the galley level.

The ship's galley is headed by the Chief Cook (Canadian) or Steward (American). The galley staff prepares three meals, breakfast, lunch and dinner, per day for the crew. A regular day for the steward begins around 6 a.m. and ends after 6 in the evening. Feeding a crew of 20 to 25 is a full-time job that requires planning, ordering supplies, making up menus, supervising the galley staff, plus cooking. S/S *Kaye E. Barker*

The Steward's Assistant, commonly referred to as the ship's porter, is the entry-level position in the galley. The porter's primary duties are to clean dishes, floors, and food preparation areas, plus help the Steward and 2nd Cook during meal preparation. In recent years the porter's position has been eliminated in some fleets with the cleaning and preparation duties being delegated to the 2nd Cook. Some Canadian vessels now operate with a one-person galley staff. M/V *American Republic*

A healthy dose of everything, and a lot of it. Cooking and food preparation is a lot like performing magic. The art of taking a variety of items and producing something wonderful to taste and eat is the mission of Great Lakes cooks. The dining experience can be like going to your favorite restaurant every night. S/S *Mississagi*

Trained as a chef at a culinary institute, Steward Don Parkington found life on the lakes more to his style than the kitchen of a posh restaurant, and he can still perform his special brand of food magic as often as he likes. S/S *Mississagi*

The 2nd Cook is responsible for the ship's baking needs...breads, rolls, and deserts. Depending upon their experience, a 2nd Cook can be a great asset in the kitchen.

Cramped, hot galley spaces were the norm for many of the older steamships. Most of those are gone, but a few remain. Regardless of their workspace, cooks on the whole are social workers and enjoy the daily comings and goings of crew and the daily banter that drifts in and out of the kitchen. ATB *Sarah Spencer*

Meal preparation goes on throughout the day in the ship's galley. Besides having a taste of good food, multi-tasking is one of the skills needed in this demanding job.

The number of women working on Great Lakes ships is slowly growing, and surprisingly not in the galley. As young women look to maritime careers they attend school to become deck officers and engineers. The employment of women in the ship's galley, however, has enjoyed a long tradition on the Great Lakes.

"I never eat like this when I go home" is a typical sailor's lament. As the baker on the ship the 2nd Cook's day begins as early as 4 or 5 a.m. getting breads into the oven, baking cookies, muffins, pies, and cakes. Many cooks shy away from pre-packaged bake goods, taking pride in preparing fresh pastry items. M/V *CSL Tadoussac*

How many ways can you prepare chicken? On the boats—the more, the better. While it is nice to have your meals prepared for you, after even 3 months on board, 3 meals a day, 7 days a week, well, you learn that variety is the spice of life. Cooks on the boats work hard to provide meals that keep the crew well fed while not getting into too much of a rut with their menus. With an older generation of workers becoming more health conscious, and a younger generation raised on fast food, the stewards have to be creative to keep everyone happy.

Dining etiquette and rules vary greatly on the ships. On most ships the 2nd Cook's still wait on the officers; on some everyone eats together. On many ships the licensed and unlicensed eat in separate areas. Cafeteria-style kitchens are also common. Crew members order from a menu posted in the dining area while dinner stays hot in the steam table.

What does it take to feed a hungry ship's crew? A lot! Stewards usually place an order of supplies every 7 to 10 days, depending upon where the ship is heading. In the spring or winter they may stock more in case they are stuck in the ice for any length of time.

The holiday Christmas tree tucked in the corner of the officers dining room can look rather lonely at 2 a.m. while the ship is loading at a cold, windswept ore dock. Holidays away from home are no different on a ship than in any job; they're difficult for many. Galley staffs around the Great Lakes try to make holiday meals something special and spend days preparing for these occasions.

- Appetizers -
Punch – Shrimp Cocktail – Deviled Eggs – Oyster Stew
Vegetable Tray with Ranch Dip

- Entrees -
Roast Long Island Duckling – Cranberry Sauce
Roast Goose – Fried Chicken
Roast Turkey – Homemade Dressing
Baked Cornish Hens – Baked Ham
Prime Rib of Beef with Au Jus
Plain or Giblet Gravy

- Vegetables -
Mashed Potatoes – Candied Sweet Potatoes
Baked Acorn Squash – Sweet Green Peas

Special holiday menu from the olden days of steam boating on the lakes.

The holiday menu from the steamer *Wilfred Sykes* carries on the tradition of fine holiday dining on the lakes.

Sample of menu items from the *E. M. Ford* Thanksgiving Day dinner menu.

Christmas tree on the steamer *Herbert C. Jackson*.

The steward dishes out a hot seafood bake prepared for dinner on the *J. W. Shelley*.

Most stewards try to keep a supply of food on board that will cover several weeks. Grocery orders are usually put in every 7 to 10 days. So, what does it take to feed a crew? 150 pounds of potatoes, 30 pounds of French fries, 20 pounds of onion rings, 15 pounds of rice, 50 pounds of flour, about 35 dozen eggs every two weeks, 30 pounds of bacon, 20 pounds of coffee, and over 40 gallons of milk. The kitchens are equipped with cold, frozen, and dry storage. Whatever food items you would be likely to find on the menu of your favorite restaurant is what you will find on board a ship.

The crew's dining area is the social center of the ship. Unlicensed members dine in their own area. The daily meal choices are posted on a chalk or dry-erase board. Crew mates on the Canadian laker *Mississagi* take a break from the day's chores at fit-out to relax and catch up on the news from over the winter.

Most crews never miss eating lunch on a ship. Hot and cold sandwiches, soups, fruit, salads, and desert are standard fare on all ships. On the older style ships the dining room is back aft on the poop deck, an area with plenty of daylight and usually air conditioned with a cool lake breeze.

One of the few holdovers from the old days on Great Lakes ships can be found in the dining areas. Licensed members of the crew, deck officers and engineers dine in a separate room from the unlicensed crew. The food is the same but the table settings are more formal for certain occasions, such as holidays. M/V *Indiana Harbor*

CHAPTER 6:
Mariners Gallery

The St. Lawrence Seaway System stretches over two thousand miles into the heart of the North American continent. Quebec City is the transition point where the fresh water descending from the Great Lakes to sea level mingles with salt water. The Port of Quebec is a major terminus for Lake Superior iron ore and grains from the American and Canadian prairies. M/V *Algoisle*

The shipping season runs from mid-March until mid-January. M/V *Burns Harbor*

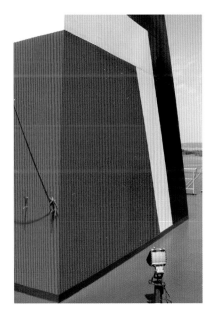

A vessel's distinctly marked smokestack is it's at-sea business card. M/V *Atlantic Erie*

Great Lakes vessel captains and mates are licensed pilots for the waters of the Great Lakes. Licensure requires hours of navigation in the rivers and the open waters before obtaining full certification. On the St. Lawrence Seaway pilotage is mandatory in three locations regardless of the master's qualifications.

M/V *American Republic* in Fox River at Green Bay.

Paul R. Tregurtha rides into a foggy sunset on Lake Superior.

The *CSL Tadoussac*, operated by Canada Steamship Lines, pushes a swell of water along its deeply laden hull as it heads down the Detroit River. While the ship is in American waters it will fly the American flag from its forward mast as a courtesy to the country where its hull is wetted. M/V *CSL Tadoussac*

The *Maritime Trader* passes beneath several bridge spans as it enters Hamilton, Ontario, for a load of soybeans. The Burlington Ship Canal separates Hamilton's harbor from Lake Ontario and is replete with a vintage stone lighthouse and two pier lights that mark the entrance to the canal.

Steam billows from the port whistle on the *Kaye E. Barker*. When operating in dense fog, ships are required to sound their whistle every few minutes as a warning to smaller craft in the vicinity that a freighter is approaching. Sustained fog can make sleeping in the after cabins beneath the stack difficult. S/S *Kaye E. Barker*

The sight of flatbacks like the *Quebecois* is becoming rarer with each passing year. Changes in the Canadian grain trade have resulted in a large shift of movement away from the Great Lakes to ports on the West Coast, and via rail traffic to the Canadian east coast. The *Quebecois* is entering Duluth to take a load of grain.

The use of self-unloading technology dominates the Canadian Great Lakes. The *Algosteel* enters the pool between the locks at Beauharnois with a load of Labrador ore. A common, non-commercial criticism of Canadian self-unloaders is often pointed at their unaesthetic unloading system housings just forward of the after cabins. The large gray metal boxes obliterate the lines of the vessels in spite of their functionality.

Ship owners are much less sentimental about their vessels than the general public. From the days of the scow schooner to today's retrofitted steamer hulls, the articulated tug-barge is a utilitarian trend that will continue to redefine shipping on the lakes as existing vessels age and laws impacting the pollutants emitted from older steam and diesel engines evolve. ATB *James L. Kuber*